More Praise for *Extraordinary Groups*

"*Extraordinary Groups* is an extraordinary book. Geoff Bellman and Kathleen Ryan have rigorously examined the compelling cases of sixty high-performing groups and revealed the elements of their success. This book is rich with uplifting stories that will inspire you, practical advice that will guide you, and applied exercises that will develop you and your team. If you want to know what is required of you to do truly amazing work in groups, then this is the place to start. Buy it now. Use it often."

—Jim Kouzes, award-winning coauthor of the bestselling book, *The Leadership Challenge*, and Dean's Executive Professor of Leadership, Leavey School of Business, Santa Clara University

"This book offers a useful model for being a great group leader or member—no small undertaking. Groups are the essential structure for making a difference in the world and this book adds to our capacity to create something important together. An easy read with a clear structure; I happily recommend it."

—Peter Block, partner, Designed Learning, and author of *Community: The Structure of Belonging*

"This is a must-read for leaders looking to achieve transformational results in their organizations. The authors not only make a compelling case about the power of engaging small groups, they give us a pragmatic blueprint to move groups to ever higher levels of performance."

—Phyllis Campbell, chairman, JPMorgan Chase, Pacific NW, and former CEO, The Seattle Foundation

"Organizational leaders will appreciate Bellman and Ryan's approach for igniting energy in group process, adding value to the business, effectively and quickly."

—Barbara Magusin, senior vice president, Human Resources, Premera Blue Cross

"In fifty years of consulting and facilitating, never has a book about groups so completely captured my interest or provoked such deep reflection and insight as *Extraordinary Groups*. Geoff Bellman and Kathleen Ryan not only capture the magic each of us feels in the presence of a deeply fulfilling group experience, but they also provide a map of the territory that can be followed by anyone seeking to create such experiences. Their work is firmly grounded in the observations and reflections of sixty members of extraordinary groups, from which they have distilled guidelines for success that are clear and doable without being overly simplistic. Their accompanying exercises can be used by anyone, whether group leader, facilitator, or member, to enhance their own experience of group life, and to help their group be all it can be—both in its impact on events in the world and in providing satisfaction for the needs we all bring to group life."

—Roger Harrison, consultant, author, and adjunct professor,
California Institute of Integral Studies

"'I am me not only because of who I am but also because I am in relation-ship.' In Archbishop Tutu's philosophy, this view of us in relationship is a fundamental life force—especially relevant in these times of 'six degrees of separation.' *Extraordinary Groups* provides a blueprint for building the rela-tionships that must occur as we find the synergies needed for problem solving and breakthrough."

—Patricia McLagan, chair, Desmond Tutu Peace Foundation

"At a time when every organization is looking for ways to inspire people, achieve more results, and build loyalty, *Extraordinary Groups* provides the way. The authors' ability to capture practical techniques coupled with ideas on how to tap into people's real desire to contribute is astonishing. A must-read for anyone interested in change and contribution."

—Carol Vipperman, president and founder,
Foundation for Russian American Economic Cooperation

"At last the book that answers how to get that 'special sauce' that makes some groups exceed our expectations while others fall so short. It provides new insights through powerful stories, practical guidance, and an essen-tial reminder of the ingredients that differentiate the ordinary from the extraordinary!"

—Ann A. Herrmann-Nehdi, CEO, Herrmann International

"Anyone charged with leadership for a project, team, or entire enterprise will be energized by this clear guide to providing outstanding outcomes through proven team tools. Amidst many works on teams, this book emerges filled with clear and try-it-today methods to produce great outcomes through super teams."

—M. Jane Dailey, vice president and chief clinical officer,
Kindred Healthcare, East Region

"Lively stories, generative questions, and practical insights support tools that cut beneath the surface of groups. Bellman and Ryan invite us to mine our own experience, to learn from what we already know, and recognize it for the first time. Coaches, managers, and leaders who want to make a difference will find *Extraordinary Groups* invaluable for staff meetings, leadership workshops, and consultations."

—Laurent A. Parks Daloz, senior fellow, The Whidbey Institute

"*Extraordinary Groups* is an original meditation and celebration of the importance of groups and teams not only in business but in our lives overall. It not only synthesizes years of research and experience with why groups succeed or fail but offers page after page of practical ideas and exercises for how to use these insights with any organized group. It is useful to both the beginner group facilitator and organizer as well as the experienced practitioners."

—David Giber, senior vice president, Linkage, Inc.

"Change gets its legs when kindred spirits bond in a common purpose. In *Extraordinary Groups* Bellman and Ryan shed light on this essential, nonlinear, relationship-based process. If you seek change, this book lends insight into an important aspect—creating teams that work."

—Peggy Holman, coauthor, *The Change Handbook*

"This book is about more than groups—it's about understanding how humans interact and make decisions. In our interconnected and increasingly collaborative world, this is essential learning for individuals and organizations that expect to deliver outcomes that exceed expectations."

—Colin Moseley, chairman, Simpson Investment Company

"Carl Rogers once said that the predictable response of individuals who feel fully and deeply heard is that 'the spine will tingle and the eyes will water!' *Extraordinary Groups* is for those of us who want to have that kind of experience on a regular basis through membership in passionate and powerfully productive groups. It is about understanding and appreciating what goes on at the intersection of transformative learning, peak experiences, high-performing teams, and the sustainable pursuit of meaningful work. The book offers an elegantly simple mosaic for perceiving and intervening in the ongoing life of groups that matter the most."

—Edie Seashore, MA, organization consultant,
and Charlie Seashore, professor, Fielding Graduate University

"Over the years we've wondered why it is that some groups are dynamic and life-giving while others are so-so, missing some kind of essential spark and failing to meet our hopes and expectations. When the latter happens, we sometimes blame ourselves, the group, or throw up our hands and blame the misaligned planets! Enter this book, combining inspiring examples, thoughtful analysis, and clear guidance about conditions that contribute to transformational work in small groups for the individuals involved as well as for the task at hand. What a timely, hopeful, and helpful resource!"

—Marcy Jackson and Rick Jackson, co-directors,
Center for Courage & Renewal

"Geoff Bellman and Kathleen Ryan have put together an engaging treatise on what makes for extraordinary teams. They eloquently take a very complex subject and boil it down to its most meaningful parts, all supported by stimulating real-world stories. I found the book to be pragmatic and backed by field research. In a nutshell, this extraordinary book should achieve amazing results."

—Stephen L. Cohen, Ph.D., senior vice president,
Global Solutions Management, Right Management

"*Extraordinary Groups* is the 21st century knowledge worker's survival guide. It reminds us that we are better together and explains how we can make ecstatic work experiences a best practice rather than a once-in-a-lifetime, bitter-sweet memory."

—Bill Koenig, administrative director, Organization Systems Renewal
Graduate Program, Seattle University

"'Life is too short to spend time in groups that do not fulfill their promise.' So say Geoff Bellman and Kathleen Ryan, who have studied sixty extraordinary groups in variety of settings. In doing so they have identified six human needs that when met increase the likelihood of extraordinary things happing. Written with sensitivity and deep understanding of the human condition, *Extraordinary Groups* is for people who are weary but not defeated by groups where both individuals and groups fall short of their true potential. *Extraordinary Groups* is destined to become a trusty guide for people who want to make a difference in their community, at work, or at home."

—Richard Axelrod, author, *Terms of Engagement: Changing the Way We Change Organizations*

"We're all part of so many groups—at work, home, and play. But when was the last time you shouted out, 'Wow, we're amazing!' about a group you were in? If it's been a while (or even never happened at all), it's high time to raise the bar. Read on and learn how to create extraordinary once-in-a-lifetime group experiences every day. Go ahead. You deserve it!"

—Robert "Jake" Jacobs, author of *Real Time Strategic Change* and *You Don't Have to Do It Alone*

"For years, we've talked about the potential power of groups and teams and their ability to transform our organizations, our communities, and our world. In *Extraordinary Groups*, Bellman and Ryan show leaders what's behind this power and offer practical advice and methods for fostering a team's abilities to achieve amazing results."

—Kim Wells, organization development advisor, Fred Hutchinson Cancer Research Center

"As a manager of small groups for over twenty-five years, the results of Bellman and Ryan's interviews gave me new ideas, practical actions, and a profound model. I found their exercises new, unique, and transformational. Do this work with your group and it will become more effective, rewarding, and fun!"

—Kevin Coray, managing partner, Coray Gurnitz Consulting

"Given the time we spend in groups you'd think we'd all be experts. Yet most groups are pretty ordinary or less. *Extraordinary Groups* provides a picture of what greatness can be, a road map to take you there, and a toolbox to make adjustments along the route. I think it is terrific!"

—Chip R. Bell, coauthor, *Take Their Breath Away*

"Successful coaches, CEOs, and business owners know that they win when they engage not only the heads but also the hearts of their teams. Bellman and Ryan show us how. Read this book if you want extraordinary results."

—Jeff Blancett, principal, the Galena Group

"Based on past experiences, most of us assume that our participation in groups will be painful, boring, and disappointing. If we ever have a positive group experience, we are amazed and grateful but assume it was a lucky happenstance. Bellman and Ryan have discovered otherwise. Based on extensive interviews about unusually successful and satisfying group experiences, they have identified and distilled the key factors that consistently lead to outstanding groups. They provide numerous examples and practical, actionable guidelines for creating group experiences that achieve high goals, and engage participants in productive—even transformative—ways. I enthusiastically recommend this book to anyone who has the ambition to make any group situation an outstanding experience for all participants. Yes, you can!"

—Saul Eisen, Ph.D., consultant, Developing Human Systems

"In *Extraordinary Groups*, Bellman and Ryan offer excellent perspectives based on solid research. Their findings support the work we have been doing internally at Microsoft around leadership teams and their effectiveness."

—Kathy Falzetta, organization development director, Microsoft

Other books by Geoff Bellman

*The Consultant's Calling: Bringing
Who You Are to What You Do*

Getting Things Done When You Are Not in Charge

*The Beauty of the Beast: Breathing
New Life into Organizations*

*Your Signature Path: Gaining New
Perspectives on Life and Work*

The Quest for Staff Leadership

Other books by Kathleen Ryan

*Driving Fear Out of the Workplace: Creating the
High-Trust, High-Performance Organization*

*The Courageous Messenger: How to Successfully
Speak Up at Work*

Extraordinary Groups

Extraordinary Groups

How Ordinary Teams Achieve Amazing Results

Geoffrey M. Bellman

Kathleen D. Ryan

JOSSEY-BASS
A Wiley Imprint
www.josseybass.com

Published by Jossey-Bass
A Wiley Imprint
989 Market Street, San Francisco, CA 94103-1741—www.josseybass.com

Readers should be aware that Internet Web sites offered as citations and/or sources for further information may have changed or disappeared between the time this was written and when it is read.

Limit of Liability/Disclaimer of Warranty: While the publisher and author have used their best efforts in preparing this book, they make no representations or warranties with respect to the accuracy or completeness of the contents of this book and specifically disclaim any implied warranties of merchantability or fitness for a particular purpose. No warranty may be created or extended by sales representatives or written sales materials. The advice and strategies contained herein may not be suitable for your situation. You should consult with a professional where appropriate. Neither the publisher nor author shall be liable for any loss of profit or any other commercial damages, including but not limited to special, incidental, consequential, or other damages.

Jossey-Bass books and products are available through most bookstores. To contact Jossey-Bass directly call our Customer Care Department within the U.S. at 800-956-7739, outside the U.S. at 317-572-3986, or fax 317-572-4002.

Jossey-Bass also publishes its books in a variety of electronic formats. Some content that appears in print may not be available in electronic books.

Library of Congress Cataloging-in-Publication Data
Bellman, Geoffrey M., 1938-
  Extraordinary groups : how ordinary teams achieve amazing results/Geoffrey M. Bellman, Kathleen D. Ryan.
      p. cm.
  Includes index.
  ISBN 978-0-470-40481-2 (cloth)
  1. Small groups.   2. Organizational change.   3. Teams in the workplace.
4. Social group work.   I. Ryan, Kathleen, 1947-   I I. Title.
  HM736.B45 2009
  302.3'4—dc22

                                                                    2009021544

Printed in the United States of America
FIRST EDITION
HB Printing   10 9 8 7 6 5 4 3 2 1

Contents

To
"The Keepers of the Flame,"
that extraordinary group leading
the Community Consulting Partnership
since 1996.
This book is for and about you.

Extraordinary Groups

Part One

OVERVIEW

1

WHY SMALL GROUPS ARE IMPORTANT NOW

Do you spend lots of time working in groups?

Are you frequently frustrated that groups are not more alive, more fulfilling, more productive?

Have you found yourself thinking, What a waste of time! Or, nobody listens! We never talk about what's important! I had really hoped to learn something here! We are so out of touch with each other! It takes us forever to do anything!

Affirmative answers to these questions suggest this book is for you.

Most of us find ourselves in groups in all aspects of our lives: teams, committees, task forces, clusters, pods, clubs, networks, boards, or councils. Regardless of what they are called, many fall short of their full potential. Plans are implemented half-way, if at all. Group members' talents and knowledge are only partially tapped. The work of the group does little to expand members' learning or sense of possibility. Interaction among members shows only periodic flashes of energy, creativity, or authentic connection.

Occasionally, we are involved in a group that transforms us, is "inspiring," "exciting," "life-changing," or "amazing." When our next group experience falls short of fantastic, we ask ourselves: What was different about that amazing group? What allowed us to work together so beautifully, so productively? How could I replicate that experience?"

The two of us have been living, watching, advising, facilitating, and leading groups for a combined total of ninety
years. Each of us has written and taught others about groups
and how to work with them. And we share the experience
of one extraordinary group: The Community Consulting
Partnership (CCP)—the group to which we have dedicated
this book. Fourteen years ago, a handful of us founded CCP,
and it has turned out to be extraordinary. Nine volunteers
run this little organization. CCP helps create more successful
not-for-profit organizations in our community while building
consulting skills in citizens. We have learned much watching
CCP evolve in purpose and structure, relationship and performance. Because of our participation in this group, each of us
has been changed for the better.

Like so many people, we have been both excited and mys-
tified by a handful of our own group experiences—those that
transcend the normal and stand out as amazing. Three years
ago, our curiosity pushed us into conversations about three
questions: Why do some groups describe themselves in such
exceptional terms, while most do not? What do these great
groups have in common that sorts them from the rest? What
might be done to create their extraordinary results more
often? That's when we decided to write this book.

Learning from the Experiences of Others

We began by going to the field and learning from others.
From the beginning, people readily shared their remarkable
group experiences with us. We discovered that extraordinary
group experiences are widely known, seldom studied, and
people want more of them! We sought out people from sixty
different groups, people of ages from seventeen to seventy
who declared they had been a part of amazing groups. They

told of groups in major corporations or institutions where people came together to streamline processes, better serve customers, save money or increase profitability. Other stories came from community or volunteer efforts, involving projects such as helping high school students improve their job interviewing skills, cleaning up neighborhoods, or building a new library. Quite another set of groups were more personal in nature, such as a group of family and friends that supported a dying woman and her children, or a women's book club, or a couple who recommitted to their marriage. And several of these groups—in all categories—relied heavily on technology to communicate or accomplish their goals.

Throughout this field study, we focused on stories in which groups of two to twenty came together and fulfilled the following conditions:

- The experience and the results achieved or surpassed expectations
- Those involved described what happened with words such as "wow," "a big win," "huge," "surprising," "meaningful," or "amazing"
- The setting was within the workplace, volunteer activities, family, or spiritual or personal growth communities
- The circumstances were face-to-face or virtual; if virtual, at least 75% of the group connection and interaction was accomplished through technology

In each conversation, we searched for what sits below the amazing experiences people talked with us about. As our ideas and model developed, we shared them in conferences and workshops. The perspectives of over 600 executives, managers, and consultants helped shape our point of view. Our conclusion: exceptional experiences can be thoughtfully nurtured and intentionally encouraged. We came to understand the dynamics of these groups, their impact, and what to do to increase the likelihood that they will occur. We share all of this in the pages ahead.

What Is an Extraordinary Group Experience?

When it comes to recognizing an extraordinary group, the old adage of "you'll know it when you see it" comes to mind—except that in this situation, it may be more of a case of "you'll know it when you *feel* it!" People instinctively sense when a group experience is something special, something different from the ordinary, something that surpasses their expectations in a positive, remarkable, and hard-to-describe way. Here are two examples of such groups. On the surface, they are quite different, yet they share critical elements of an extraordinary group experience. As each story unfolds, put yourself in the place of those we interviewed and imagine your way into an intuitive sense of each of these exceptional groups.

Micro-Credit for Millions

In 1996 when she was newly graduated from college, Barb was one of twelve staff members hired to organize a global summit that engaged 3,000 participants from 137 countries. The purpose of this global conference in Washington, D.C. was to launch a coordinated campaign to reach 100 million of the world's poorest families with access to credit for self-employment—and all this by the year 2005. Unlike other summits of the 1990s, this one was convened by civil society—not by governments or the United Nations. Two years prior to Barb's involvement, this effort was brought to life by grassroots citizen activists committed to ending poverty. We interviewed Barb, her co-worker Jacki, and Sam, their visionary executive director.

Starting in June, 1996, the goal for the conference staff was to organize and then orchestrate this complex, politically sensitive, international multiday event that would take place eight months later. As a small example of the challenge they took on together, Barb remembers "trying not to panic when I had the White House on one line, the First Lady of Angola on another, and the president of Peru trying to call in all at the same time. Where was Emily Post's book of protocol and etiquette on pecking order when I needed it?!" Operating out of a very tight office space—actually an old converted apartment building—"people came from all over the country to be involved. We were very eclectic." They brought different ethnic backgrounds, personalities, cultural perspectives, education, professional identities, language skills, and reasons for being involved.

At minimum pay, they often worked eighteen-hour days managing the details of everything: coordinating security for visiting heads of state, lining up conference speakers, and making sure that there were enough copies of the program when, three days before the conference, registrations jumped from 1,600 to 3,000. At all hours, staff members worked the phones in multiple languages to secure the participation of key leaders from around the globe and their personal commitments to take action once the conference was over. With solid funding, Jacki remembers that "our biggest problem was that no one had heard of micro-credit." Once people understood what it was, "everyone thought what we were doing was terrific and pitched in to help."

Conflicts occurred "when we were tired and hungry and had not gotten enough sleep." With only two private offices, staff members gathered in one to sort things out. As an organization, "it was not hugely hierarchical—people were expected to come forward. Everything seemed to get an airing." With a just-do-it attitude and respect for one another, "we'd work really hard, vent when we needed to, and then go out for a dinner or a drink together." Jacki told us that "it was war. Us against poverty—and we had each others' backs." When the conference closed as a huge success, many of the staff ended up at one person's apartment. "We couldn't leave each other for a couple of days. How could we possibly disband? We had bonded for life."

The team that put on the Micro-Credit Summit produced results that are amazing and transforming on multiple levels. When they began, they had hoped for 600 participants and 3,000 came! And more important, all delegates had agreed to the conference's goals and made commitments about micro-credit loans prior to arriving for the meeting. Careful tracking of the commitments to extending the micro-credit revealed that it took two years longer than originally targeted to achieve the conference's goals. But when reached, what an achievement! "This is a tremendous achievement that many people thought was far too difficult to reach. What makes it even more remarkable is that loans to more than 100 million very poor families now touch the lives of more than half a billion family members around the world. That is half of the world's poorest people."[1]

In addition to this astonishing global accomplishment, Jacki and Barb were deeply affected personally as members of this group. For Jacki, this was "one of the most important moments of my life . . . I'm now fearless when it comes to asking anyone for anything." Barb speaks poignantly of a transformational moment that took place at the very end of the conference. Back stage, looking out at the 3,000 people in the auditorium, she saw that "In the front row with queens and first ladies and heads of state, one person stood, then two others stood, arm in arm, singing our closing song. Then I saw an ocean of people standing up, arm in arm, and singing. I realized that in this room alone, we had the resources that could make our vision happen. My heart was blown open with deep appreciation and hope and a sense that I could make a difference. We were a squad of twelve people! In a disheveled office. Our small voice engaged the world. I could never be the same again." Hold this in mind as you read about Laura.

A Moving Experience

Twenty years ago Laura worked in information technology at a large advertising agency in New York City. She recalls the moment she was told she would be working eight weekends in a row, "I was less than excited. I thought that this was going to be a miserable two months. I couldn't have been more wrong . . . It was a very powerful experience. At the time, I didn't see it as transformative, but now I do. I try to emulate what we did then. I use it as my model for beautiful planning and collaboration."

Unlike the enormous scope of Barb's group, Laura and her nine colleagues were tasked with a very immediate mission: disconnect then reinstall the electronic equipment of employees on sixteen floors, moving from an old building to a new one across town. Transfer two floors a week, beginning each Friday morning, completing by Sunday night. Do so with a level of accuracy that would allow employees to be at their work stations on Monday morning with all phones, computers, printers, copiers, and fax machines working. Without a hitch. And, in fact, that's what happened.

Proudly, Laura recalls that "we had a 99+ percent success rate—fewer than 1 percent voiced complaints on Monday mornings." Careful planning and organization, clear goals and roles allowed the moving team to excel both individually and collectively. "We each knew what we were supposed to do so we could go ahead and make our own decisions about how to get our work accomplished." People would do their own jobs, then move on to help others in "true collaboration." One night, the printers wouldn't work consistently. The whole team pitched in and finally got them working perfectly. "We had this unspoken rule that if one of our subgroups was having a problem we all stayed to help. No one went home earlier than the others saying 'my part is done.'"

Picture this high-performing group. Already putting in a full week's work, they'd start on Friday mornings, work til 2 A.M. Saturday, then come back around 10 A.M. and work til after midnight. "We worked til 2 A.M. in order to have the rest of Sunday off," Laura explained. For eight weeks. Imagine the office floors in the new building, filled with only empty work stations. Then the high-energy team arrives, focused individuals moving from task to task, helping others wherever needed. Learning each other's favorite foods to order in. Playing baseball with broom sticks and paper wads in the middle of the night to let off steam. Then, in the early morning hours, waiting to make sure everyone was safely on their way home.

With each floor, there were different technical challenges. "For the first few weeks it was exciting. At weeks five and six, we still had the same level of commitment—and we were better at it!" A competent and caring leader helped make the project fun and gave people confidence. "We never had to deal with negative attitude—even though there were plenty of frustrations that people faced individually." Looking back on the repetitive installations, the long and late hours, and the spurts of intensely focused problem solving, Laura sees that "there was pure joy in doing something hard—together. The magic was in the group. This was a happy surprise—that it went so smoothly and was really fun!"

Defining Extraordinary Groups

Barb's and Laura's experiences are quite different in terms of the scope of their groups' goals and achievements. Yet they have several elements in common that mark them as members of two extraordinary groups. Consider their experiences as you read these definitions:

- A *group* is a collection of individuals, typically of two to about twenty, who come together around a common purpose.
- *Extraordinary groups* achieve outstanding results, and members—individually or collectively—experience a profound shift in how they see their world; they are transformed.
- *Transformation* is a fundamental shift in individual perceptions that accelerate behavior change and personal vitality.

When there is a shift in perception, things are never quite the same again. Barb and Laura each worked with about a dozen people in a very concentrated, intense, and time-driven way. For Barb, the transformative shift had to do with seeing herself as capable of making a difference in the world. Laura gained a model for joy-filled planning and collaboration.

However large or small, visible or intangible, such transformative shifts happen because the group experience satisfies core needs that members intuitively bring to any group they join. Each of us brings these same needs to every group situation; we seek opportunities to meet those needs. Our work and our field study suggest there are six needs, forming three pairs related to one's self, the group, and the world in which the group exists. These six elements combine in a model we call the Group Needs model:

Acceptance of self while moving toward one's *Potential*

A *Bond* with others that grows while pursuing a common *Purpose*

Understanding the *Reality* of the world while collectively making an *Impact*

Whether at work, at home, or in the community, when your group experience meets two or more of these needs, it will stand out for you. You are more likely to exclaim about it, to see it as memorable, and you will also find it hard to describe. You will probably be uncertain about how it came about, perhaps see it as "chance," and assume that this unusual occurrence cannot be intentionally created. Our experience suggests otherwise.

What to Expect from *Extraordinary Groups*

In the following chapters, we explain our Group Needs model in detail, share stories of extraordinary groups in action, and offer guidance to help you encourage extraordinary experiences in your groups. This book comes in three parts.

Part One: We present an overview of the key elements of our model, including the defining indicators of an extraordinary group and the connection between the Group Needs model and transformation.

Part Two: Each pair of the Group Needs model is described in its own chapter along with reflective exercises and suggestions for actions you can take in your groups to increase the chances of the six Group Needs being met. Chapter Seven illustrates transformative shifts that occur when multiple needs are met at once.

Part Three: In this section, we offer specific content on how to embrace differences within a group so that they become an asset rather than a barrier to success. We provide special guidance to group leaders, then bring the book to a close with a final chapter.

Appendices: Here you will find content that will help you apply all that we propose in the main part of the book: exercises to practice what you learn in Chapters Four, Five, and Six; a summary of the key content points; a list that describes how we intentionally behaved toward one another during our collaboration to ensure an extraordinary experience; and intriguing references about related topics.

We have written *Extraordinary Groups* to help you see your groups differently. So that you can consciously behave in ways that will encourage your groups to be extraordinary. This is possible regardless of your role: member, designated leader, or facilitator of a group. From our interviews, we'll provide twenty inspiring examples from amazing groups, groups that have much in common. Some of the stories will reflect the experiences of ongoing groups; others describe one-time events or projects. You'll find a small version of our Group Needs model in the margin next to each story we share. We also talk to you directly, asking you to do your own thinking about what we present. Please engage with us by practicing what you read. Keep track of your learning in a journal or notebook. If you do, reading *Extraordinary Groups* could become a powerful—even transformative—experience for you.

Why Are Small Groups So Important Now?

Margaret Mead's famous exhortation speaks to us: "Never doubt that a small group of thoughtful, committed people can change the world. Indeed, it is the only thing that ever has." "A small group"—say two to twenty. "Committed"—to a common purpose. To "change the world"—their world. Perhaps your group and your world. But why small groups now?

Individuals regularly feel the constraints of being in organizations; organizations are regularly frustrated in dealing with individuals. The small group is the most constructive place for individuals and an organization to achieve mutual satisfaction and accomplishment. The group is the best place to resolve issues for both. The group is the meeting ground where most work gets done—at work and in our communities.

Our attraction to groups is instinctual; two hundred thousand years of human history have formed us into the group creatures that we are. We are genetically informed to look to groups to meet many of our needs; we are not informed to look at organizations in that way. The deeper motivations for why we join with others are hardly touched upon in popular leadership and team literature. As a result, the tools and techniques they employ often miss and cannot touch these underlying drives.

Readers do not need yet another book about improving groups through team building, leadership training, or meeting management. As helpful as all those books have been, they bring us tools that only scratch the surface of the world we live in. We need to dig deeper, into the wants, needs, and motives that cause people to work together. How do we capture the energy flowing from people trying to meet their needs, rather than shut it off? How might we direct all that power? What work, paid or volunteer, lends itself to capturing that energy for the benefit of all? We think small groups are a logical place to demonstrate the answers to these questions. Currently, they are underappreciated, underutilized—and essential to work and play, family and community life.

The world currently reels with the weight of enormous challenges: wars, financial crisis, collapsing institutions, record unemployment, and climate change. All big, all global, all systemic. All requiring many perspectives, collaborative effort, and shared commitment from the global to the local level. When it comes to making progress on such issues, large organizations have regularly been found lacking; we are still learning better ways of bringing people together than by working within hierarchy and silos. In this book, we propose that human beings function better on a scale they can understand and influence—small groups that bring the right people together in the right ways can meet the challenges before us.

For organizations and individuals, we see many benefits to paying attention to creating exceptional group experiences— and then taking action to make more groups come alive like Laura's and Barb's. Organizations benefit from intentional development of peak group experiences because

- Goals set for groups are achieved and frequently surpassed
- Group performance releases talent and energy not usually available to the organization
- People develop superior skills, knowledge, and insight together, thereby increasing the capacity of the organization
- Enduring relationships and networks grow and set the stage for future collaborations

- Loyalty to the organization increases along with the sense that "this is a great place to work"

For individuals, the benefits are powerful and personal. Through extraordinary experiences with others, individuals find

- Increased confidence in their abilities and performance
- Higher motivation and morale
- Restored faith in and increased appreciation for organizations
- New and deeper connections with others
- New skills and knowledge that lead to a larger sense of personal empowerment
- Individual effort that is both rewarded and multiplied by working in groups

All of this leads the two of us to a clear point of view: Life is too short to spend time in groups that do not fulfill their promise. Our own personal lives and years of consulting have shown us that everyone benefits when people experience the pride, energy, and fulfillment that come from being part of an extraordinary group. Anyone in a group, regardless of role, can help move that group toward a transformative, never-to-be-forgotten experience. Extraordinary groups may be the exception, but they are widely experienced and largely unexamined. The two of us want to change that and we invite you to join us in this effort.

Notes

1. Mohammad Yunus. *MicroCredit Summit Newsletter*, January, 2009. Vol. 7, Issue 1.

2

WHAT'S DIFFERENT ABOUT EXTRAORDINARY GROUPS

An extraordinary group *achieves outstanding results while members experience a profound shift in how they see their world.* These amazing groups show up in all sectors, they pursue all manner of purposes. Our sixty stories of these extraordinary groups came from organization leaders, information technology professionals, soldiers, software developers, trainers, managers, human resource officers, small business owners, community college counselors, basketball coaches, high school teachers, doctors, nurses, event organizers, community activists, health care administrators, consultants, soccer players, parishioners insurance executives, community volunteers, moms, government contractors, philanthropists, ministers high school students, book club members, white-water rafters, motorcycle riders, barbershop quartet singers, board members . . .

We examined sixty wonderfully different groups that shared a common enthusiasm for their "extraordinariness." We asked ourselves what *extraordinary* means, what indicators sort these amazing groups from the all the rest, what features differentiate these "Wow!" groups from all those that are "OK, but not great." In this chapter, we share our findings with you, and use one such group to illustrate an extraordinary group in action. We encourage you to think about your groups in the context of what we have discovered about extraordinary groups.

What Distinguishes an Extraordinary Group?

Our field study yielded eight indicators linked to what we are calling "extraordinary." Watch an extraordinary group and you will see these eight indicators in action. Barb's and Laura's groups had most of them, and so did most of sixty groups we studied.

Extraordinary groups exhibit

- A *compelling purpose* that inspires and stretches members to make the group and its work a top priority
- *Shared leadership* that encourages members to take mutual responsibility for helping the group be successful
- *Just-enough-structure* to create confidence to move forward, but not so much as to become bureaucratic or burdensome
- *Full engagement* that results in all members jumping in with enthusiasm, sometimes passionately and chaotically, regardless of role
- *Embracing differences* so that group members see, value, and use their diversity as a strength
- *Unexpected learning* that translates into personal and group growth
- *Strengthened relationships* among members characterized by trust, collegiality, and friendship
- *Great results*, tangible and intangible

Keep this list of indicators at hand. Watch an extraordinary group at work and you will be busy checking them off. You will see one indicator after another, often many at once, bouncing off and building upon one another. As we interviewed people, these eight themes surfaced again and again.

Whether the groups were for profit or not, involving volunteers or employees, face-to-face or virtual, these eight indicators emerged. Not every story illustrated every point, but every story contained several.

We use one story, Tom's team of seven people, to illustrate the indicators. You will see how one person felt a need, initiated action, pressed a point, and brought a team together to get something done.

Bucking the System

Years ago, Tom, a young information technology executive, returned to a former employer to take a mid-management position; the company was an equipment manufacturer with many divisions. At that time, IT was totally centralized at corporate headquarters. The plan would require three smaller divisions—mining equipment, rail car, and winch manufacturing—to adopt an IT system designed for the much larger manufacturing division. This made no sense to Tom, who thought each division needed a system to match its own work, not one designed for a very different part of the company and tied to the corporate mainframe. But the decision had been made and "once something like that was decided— that was it!"

Tom's questioning of the decision was a heretical act: he challenged a decision made higher up the chain and did so outside the company's formalized budget cycle. Nonetheless, he managed to get the go-ahead to investigate an alternative approach. Six people joined him: Fred, the manager of IT planning, whom we also interviewed, a cost accounting manager, a materials manager, an assistant comptroller, an IT data processing manager, and an assistant vice-president from the corporate office "assigned to ride herd on what we were doing." Nobody formally reported to Tom and everyone already had their plates full with other assignments. But, as Fred recalls, each member who chose to be involved was "top notch and well-thought of at the company level." And each was frustrated by the company's one-system policy and the slowness with which it was being implemented.

Spread over four different locations in the West and Midwest of the United States and Canada, the team met in person quarterly, typically around some milestone or event, such as site visits to investigate software possibilities. In between, Fred recalls weekly phone meetings, remembering that this was a time well before easy Internet connections and conference calls. Tom remembers that it was a challenge just to "get everyone on the same page and believing that we could actually pull this off." Pressure was mounting for the smaller divisions to adopt the corporate system. The work of this group needed to move ahead quickly!

The group analyzed the systems' needs of the three smaller divisions. They investigated hardware, software, other companies, vendors, technical challenges, costs, and the interface with the corporate mainframe. After all their research, they recommended that the smaller divisions get midrange computers with packaged software that could be quickly installed and provide maximum flexibility for the users. In less than eight months, they went from "stirring the water to getting the sign-off" on their recommendation. Tom says, "We ended up getting corporate approval for the three divisions to each have their own system, doing the first implementation in one year. The total projected cost was $6.5 million for the four divisions, including putting IT people in the divisions. We brought our first division in on time and under budget. In one division alone, the new system was responsible for $1 million savings on a yearly basis."

An Amazing Group at Work

Tom and Fred's group illustrates the unique qualities exhibited in extraordinary groups. Initially it was tempting to try to arrange these eight indicators into some kind of linear flow. We came to see that in real-life these elements flow back and forth synergistically, depending on the way in which group members interact with one another. You might think of these indicators as the right ingredients to make a fabulous soup. Separately, they are appealing but when combined and given time to simmer in the same pot, they create something extraordinary and far more memorable than what could have been produced without the time to blend their separate flavors.

As you read through these eight descriptions, think about one of your groups. How often do you see or experience these qualities? When you do, how do they influence your experience?

Compelling Purpose

Watch an extraordinary group at work and you will see that an inspiring and shared purpose surfaces repeatedly. Motivated by their purpose, members make their group a priority even in the face of other demands on their time. Members know that agreeing on a common purpose is critical to their work together. They make purpose visible, they post it, they remind each other of it, they use it as their primary guide for decisions. They check with each other when they suspect that purpose is not commonly understood.

A clear, compelling purpose is easy to see in task-oriented groups, ones we call External Change groups. For them, doable goals that require a stretch are important and set in motion action plans, work assignments, and

deadlines. Most groups brought together in the work environment have this type of purpose. For example, Tom and
Fred's team came together to analyze the information system's needs and to shape a recommendation. At the more
compelling level, what they were really about was trying to
do what was right for one portion of the business—and they
took no small satisfaction in bucking the top-down system
at the same time. Tom remembers that "the others were
interested in getting involved. They got caught up in the
possibility of doing something that made sense and going
against the centralized bull. They liked the idea of breaking
that mold."

Purpose is equally important to more socially-oriented
groups—which we call Individual Support groups. Friendship
circles that meet on regular basis, book clubs, or professional
development groups are examples. In less task-driven settings,
members are strongly drawn to their shared, internal purpose,
typically providing some type of support for one another. Just
as with external, task-driven groups, a purpose that is clear
and compelling allows the relationship-driven groups to collectively assess how they are doing at what they have come
together to achieve.

Shared Leadership

Watch an extraordinary group in action and you will notice
leadership behaviors from across the group. These groups are
not top-down or leader-centric. Instead leadership is expressed
by many in the group; the lead role shifts with the subject at
hand and the expertise required. Many groups self-organize;
members know that anyone can initiate with a question,
a task, an issue, or a proposal. In these groups, you will see
members leading together: initiating, facilitating, structuring,

suggesting, and doing all manner of things to help the group be effective. With shared leadership, members take mutual responsibility for outcomes. This gives everyone more opportunity to assist in getting what the group wants. Each member of Fred and Tom's group was a manager in his own right, some were higher on the corporate ladder than Tom, who had initiated the group. Depending on their areas of expertise, each led a different aspect of the work. For example, the materials manager coordinated with his counterparts in the three divisions, keeping people in the loop, gathering data, and moving the assessment process ahead. As decision points surfaced, members relied on each other's content expertise for guiding the group through the steps required to reach their recommendations.

This is not to suggest that extraordinary groups do not have formal leaders. They often do, but those assigned that role see their jobs differently from how more directive leaders do. How so? These leaders know their role is very important *and* that they are one leader among many. Typically, they focus on seeing that the group is being led rather than on being the one constant leader. They turn responsibilities and questions back to the group; they ask others what they would do. They pay attention to group members and try to see that individual needs are addressed.

Tom is such a leader. Even after twenty years, he can recount what each member in his group did to advance the work and how their competence and enthusiasm came together to make a great team. Aside from being the point person to buck the system, he "carried the water for the troops. You've got to organize around people's excitement and their desires and abilities to get things done. It's important to keep it light and to care about people, especially when they are overcommitted."

Just-Enough Structure

Give extraordinary groups a clear purpose and they will come up with ways of working that are governed more by outcome than structure. They will establish and honor systems, plans, roles, tasks, and working agreements—*if* those structures fit the challenges ahead of them. But they never forget that the main reason they are together is about fulfilling their purpose. The structure is a means to that end. In Tom and Fred's group, the "secret was to keep it human. We used some rudimentary project management tools—like a task list. We reviewed this in our weekly meeting and updated it together. That's the only way this sort of thing gets done. Keep it simple but make sure that everyone is informed and included."

More organic than mechanical, members work together in ways that are collaborative, flexible, creative, and adaptive. They create just-enough-structure—at the time that it is needed—to support purpose and outcomes. They guard against overstructuring or structuring too soon, both of which can impose boundaries on people's thinking and limit the time available for substantive conversations. Agendas are never more important than the outcomes they are designed to meet; roles and plans shift as circumstances call for reaching toward purpose in a new way.

Full Engagement

The space created by compelling purpose, just-enough structure, and shared leadership pulls members toward full engagement. When fully engaged, members readily contribute their knowledge, skills, and talents; they do not wait to be asked. In a group like this, rather than holding back, members may have trouble getting airtime—waiting for others to breathe so they can dive in. Depending on what's being discussed, the intensity and excitement of engagement can be more apparent than order. Ideas flow, tumbling one over another like a river just forming and seeking its course. People pitch in, adapt, inform, exclaim, and resolve issues together. And engagement doesn't end when a meeting is over; people do what they say they will do. When a member commits to taking action, others can count on that person to follow through. People work hard and intensely, often for hours, days at a time; they do so because they are committed to their unifying purpose and don't want to let each other down.

Tom and Fred's group had one of these intensely focused times. As they were conducting their due diligence on issues and finances, they knew that they were off-cycle for the company's budget process. They got the word from headquarters that the CEO of the company had finally agreed to consider the group's proposal. With this, the group had hopes they could bypass some of the normal rules and procedures. Tom remembers that "then my boss called and said 'show up tomorrow morning.' The team was completely together on this. We stayed up until 2 A.M. to get ready for the presentation the next day." When the next day came, "we were ready and we nailed it!"

Extraordinary groups thrive because members are enthusiastic and are willing to speak passionately about things that are important. Sometimes group dynamics get complicated and messy—but that's OK. Conflict and disagreement are not uncommon and are not avoided. Members give each other the benefit of the doubt and do not expect each other to be perfect communicators. Laughing, good humor, playful energy, and a joyful spirit show up—and can be present even in the face of very serious circumstances or tense moments. People take pleasure in being together with others who care about the same thing. Irreverence or spontaneous play often erupt, producing side-splitting laughter. This breaks the tension of work and gives the group a larger perspective that helps members understand that all is not seriousness and struggle. Joking and kidding are rooted in positive intent and appreciation of one another, rather than in power or competition. Fred remembers that the group members really had fun together. Tom recalls that "We frequently went down the street after work and shared a pitcher of beer. We laughed a lot and hammered out what we needed to do next. We had a good time together—and we all gained a great deal of respect for each other throughout this time."

Embracing Differences

In extraordinary groups, people are intrigued by the diversity of information, perspectives, backgrounds, and cultures within the group. They respect each other for who they are as human beings as well as for the skills, knowledge, and talent they apply to the group's purpose. Members know that creative solutions require a broad range of viewpoints and the ability to blend positions—even contradictory ones. With this frame, they experience their unique ideas being respected, listened to, and talked about in service to group purpose. Fred remembers that his group "was a true team, where everyone had input and egos didn't get in the way. There was no 'I'm doing this *my* way.'" A culture of deferring to the subject matter experts quickly developed. "Beyond deferring details to them, we developed a consensus approach for the bigger issues. We wanted to go forward with a plan that had everyone fully committed. We couldn't afford to have members of the team questioning our decisions or our decision-making process after the fact."

Respect for differences makes it easier for members to bring their true selves to the group. People feel appreciated for who they are; they know that acceptance in the group does not require them to pretend to be someone else. As a result, people are more spontaneous, more likely to take risks, and generally give expression to sides of themselves often not shown in ordinary groups. Members readily acknowledge what they don't know without apology, and what they do know without bragging.

These dynamics promote a sense of safety and trust. In safe environments, members take risks because they trust each other; they do not worry about their intentions being misinterpreted or suffering a reprisal for something they say. They challenge each other, push boundaries, work through differences, share personal stories and experiences—including ones that are painful. They discuss undiscussable[1] issues to get to the bottom of misunderstandings or hurt feelings. They give each other feedback and ask for it in return. They strive for sensitivity but not perfection in their communications because they know others will accept them for who they are. And they collaborate—willingly and openly sharing ideas, building off each others' perspectives and information, stretching toward breakthrough thinking and reaching powerful decisions together. In this way, respect, safety—and the trust that follows—allow for full engagement.

Tom remembers that "there was a high degree of mutual respect. Some of our best work came out of arguments. People felt safe defending a position and safe compromising when needed. The willingness to compromise was helped by that mutual respect. For my part, I reminded everyone that we were not trying to solve world hunger; we were simply trying to convince a conservative corporation to start doing business in a new way."

Unexpected Learning

Of course people in groups expect to learn, but our extraordinary groups were characterized by learning that went beyond their expectations. You can almost hear learning taking place in an extraordinary group. Learning is central to these groups being transformed. A phrase that captures the energy of this learning is "Ready . . . Set . . . Stretch!" The stretch extends beyond incremental growth; it is an intentional reach to become more together. It's one thing for a member to be uniquely challenged by the task; it's quite another when the entire group takes up the challenge together. Excited by the work before them, members are united in learning together and supporting one another. Often what they learn together has wider application than this project with this team; it applies in their careers and lives.

As a pattern, members of extraordinary groups give more than they originally signed up for: more hours, more energy, more expertise, more patience, more sweat, more empathy, more study, and more risk. In their stretch, members grow in real skills, knowledge, mental frameworks, awareness of self, and sense of potential. Members expand their beliefs of what a group can accomplish together—with profound implications for future groups they will join.

Time and time again, people we interviewed reported being changed, increasing personal confidence, and learning so much! Fred was one of them: "I learned lessons that I didn't know before. About how to get the right people on the team, how to work together so that egos don't get in the way, how to do a process from end-to-end." Fred left the company soon after the installation of the systems his group recommended. As his career unfolded, he told us that "I was a project leader for my whole career." The lessons gained through this team served him well for years.

Strengthened Relationships

Relationships between members of extraordinary groups take shape in two primary ways. Some groups form around established relationships; members so enjoy being together that they search for shared purpose and activity that allow them to go on spending time together. Continuing, deepening, and strengthening what they already have in their relationship is a high priority. Other groups draw together first around group purpose. As members join they meet new people, but they are initially attracted more to purpose than to each other. New relationships grow from the work together and sometimes result in lasting friendships. This is not surprising, given the quality and energy of the interactions that characterize such groups.

When group behavior causes individuals to feel respected, enhanced relationships are a natural result. Groups that help members discover common values or interests feed friendship. When the norm is to rely on one another, to commit, and to follow-through, what else would we expect? Add to this the bonds formed through facing challenges together and the fun of daily work and celebrating accomplishment. Tom says, "When we got the whole team in one place, we were together for all of our waking hours for two to three days in a row." The friendships that evolved out of such intensely focused work lasted years beyond people's tenure at the company. Even twenty plus years later, Tom knew how to reach two other members of the team so we could interview them.

Great Results

Results that surpass members' expectations regularly happen in extraordinary groups. Over two-thirds of those we interviewed identified impressive *tangible* results. With Tom's team, the operating costs for the one division alone were reduced by $1 million per year. The company's later sale of the division was possible because its information system was not tied to the corporate mainframe. Among our other groups we heard many stories of remarkable accomplishments— a library built, software developed, research completed, conferences held, strategies planned, a beach cleaned, a neighborhood beautified, candidates screened, championships won, markets gained, military missions accomplished, students sent abroad, cargo transported, and lives saved.

Even informed by results such as these, we wish we could guarantee that all the changes groups want to make in the world will be wildly successful. We can't. Why? There are simply too many intervening variables that depend on factors outside any group's span of control. For example, what if the corporate executives had said "No"—for whatever reason—to Tom and Fred's team? We are convinced, however, that by paying attention to the indicators highlighted here, members and leaders will dramatically increase the likelihood that they will achieve or exceed the tangible outcomes they seek. Looking back to our field study, four out of forty-six External Change groups were not successful at achieving their ultimate goals. In spite of this, those we interviewed still described their group experience as amazing. This judgment comes directly from valued *intangible* results of the group experience.

Results that are not readily measured in numbers, dollars, percentages, or units turn out to be tremendously important to extraordinary groups. When members speak of the amazing aspects of what they did together, with a few exceptions, the tangible results seldom make the top of their list. Why might this be? Tangible results are usually seen as an indicator of the success of what they did, not the success itself. The success itself is usually associated with the more intangible ways people worked together. Learning, increased confidence, and enhanced relationships are the most significant outcomes of these extraordinary groups. Members also glow in their pride of accomplishment or their sense of community. Dramatic testimony to the importance of the intangible came from people who had life-changing experiences. For example: altering a career path, redefining the meaning of family, experiencing a shift in self-esteem, or becoming a part of a community that helped one person stay centered and positive as she faced chronic health challenges in her family.

These intangible results transformed the lives of individual group members. After this, a person's internal experience and external view of her world are never quite the same again. After three years of studying and thinking about extraordinary groups, we know that when someone says "That was an amazing experience!" a powerful intangible shift has most likely taken place. As you will see from the stories we share in the chapters ahead, impressive tangible results usually accompany the intangible transformative shifts. But they seem to take second place to the changes in people's internal experience. A notable exception was one executive who became tangibly rich beyond his dreams. The money was very compelling and changed his life; but although his story provoked a little envy, it stood out as being one of the few in which the tangible made the most important difference.

Looking back on his experience, Tom knows that his team enabled him to make a powerful shift in how he saw himself in the world. "It gave me legitimacy. I already knew what it meant to do this kind of technological change, but this experience showed me I could rise above personal fears and redefine my success. I didn't have a history of bucking the system and I've never really liked confrontation." More than once Tom was told by his superiors to "back off." During the presentation to the CEO, the company's comptroller asked, "How confident are you that this is a good idea?" Tom replied, "I'll bet my job on it." Like Fred, Tom also left the company not long after the IT systems were installed in the three divisions. What he learned propelled him to seek leadership roles with increasing scope and responsibility; the transformative shift he described to us stayed with him and shaped his leadership throughout the years. When we spoke with him, he was president of a company.

Next we provide an overview of the elements that come together to shape an experience such as Tom's.

Notes

1. Ryan, K., and Oestreich, D. *Driving Fear Out of the Workplace: Creating the High-Trust, High-Performance Organization* (pp. 77–90). San Francisco: Jossey-Bass, 1998.

3

WHAT ORDINARY GROUPS NEED

When a group experience—like that of Tom and Fred described in Chapter Two—meets members' deep-seated, instinctive group needs, it sets a standard for groups in the future. People readily recall such experiences and describe them enthusiastically. It was "amazing," "wonderful," "hard to describe," "really something," or simply "wow!" This chapter gets beyond those vague exclamations and into the dynamics that support such zeal. Such exclamations result from individual needs being met; we explore those needs in our Group Needs model. They also represent certain feelings common to extraordinary groups; we elaborate on those. In the midst of all this is an elusive concept called "transformation"; we do our best to tie that down. Along the way through the chapter, we'll provide three illustrations from our field study. Let's begin with needs and our model before moving on to transformation and feelings.

Our Instinctive Need to Group

As human beings, we have been grouping for a very long time, hundreds of thousands of years. We have evolved interdependently; we have survived as a species by facing the future together. We know it; our genes know it. In the ancient past, we came together for protection and procreation. Today, we come together to protect our shared identity and to pursue a purpose that will move us toward the future. Yet every twenty-first-century, stylishly outfitted, color-coordinated group is informed by more "primitive" instincts. The most logical, planning-oriented, analytical project team also lives in a world of nonrational, chaotic, emotion-driven instinctive needs. Our desires for inclusion, a sense of team, and a feeling of being a part of something greater than ourselves are all examples of those intuitive longings. We bring these very human needs to every group meeting. But what do we do with these deep set needs that we typically do not think of or talk about? Answering this question begins with understanding our needs.

Six Group Needs

Here's our proposition: As individuals, we all come to groups with a set of mostly unarticulated ancient needs that we long to meet through group experiences. This is true whether the group is a recreation league sports team, a problem-solving group at work, a nonprofit board of directors, or a family gathered around the kitchen table. In the pages ahead, these longings will be referred to as Group Needs. Because they represent deeply held yearnings, they are central to who we are as human beings and reside in the core of our instinctive selves. We present these needs in three pairs:

- Self: *Acceptance* of self while moving toward one's *Potential*

- Group: A *Bond* with others that grows while pursuing a common *Purpose*
- World: Understanding the *Reality* of the world while making an *Impact*

The three pairs join and overlap, creating a synergistic and transformative effect.

The Group Needs Model

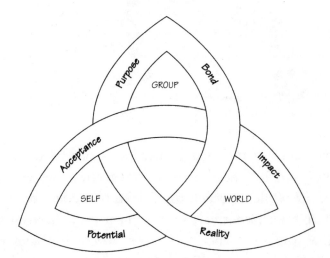

Three pairs of Group Needs form a knot of three interlaced loops. This ancient image can be traced back to 400 A.D.; its openness, continuous movement, and interconnection fit well with the interplay of the six Group Needs. We use this triple looped knot to frame how you can see the groups in your life. New possibilities reveal themselves when you see through the framework of this knot. Its six Group Needs and three loops are key to moving your group toward an extraordinary experience.

Later, in Chapters Four, Five, and Six, we explore each pair of the six needs in detail. But first, an overview of the three loops.

Self-Acceptance and Potential

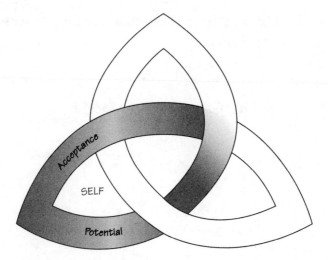

The two sides of this first loop express our need to accept ourselves and our need to become even more, embracing who we are while we reach toward who we could become. In groups we humans actively seek to meet these needs whether we know it or not, whether we can articulate them or not. They provide motives for much of what we do. Here's how we define each.

- Acceptance: Knowing and accepting ourselves for who we are.
- Potential: Sensing and growing into our fuller and better selves.

The two sides of the loop reveal the creative dynamic of simultaneously accepting ourselves in the moment and growing into our Potential. As we accept ourselves, we become more willing to step into situations that requiring us to stretch. A sense of our future selves can help us appreciate our current capabilities. Acceptance and Potential: different and inextricably linked. Consider the following example of how a group experience can help someone accept himself in the present and sharpen his Potential to make changes in the future.

One Project Leads to a New Career

Bruce worked for a large manufacturing company, quite con-tentedly developing technical training courses for front line employees. One day a request came in that changed both the direction of his career and how he saw himself at work. One of the unions asked the company for a ten-module course on basic electronics fully utilizing computer technology. This was at a time when computer-based-training was a new concept and not widely understood or used within Bruce's organization. No one individual in Bruce's work group was capable of responding to the request.

A team of four, including Bruce, was asked to assess the possibility of taking on the project. Bruce was a technical writer; his teammates included two instructional designers and one skills instructor. When they enthusiastically rec-ommended that the project move ahead, they became the implementation team. For six months, these four worked together, breaking new ground for the company. Working with a vendor, they delivered the specific course to rave reviews, helped establish the value of computer-based-training, and developed a model for how the company would partner with outside vendors for similar courses in the future. This was cutting-edge work! As Bruce looked at their accomplishments, he said, "We built the capacity of the organization, resulting in a higher-quality educational experience at a lower cost."

But our focus is on Bruce's insights into himself. Demonstrating noteworthy self-Acceptance, he candidly told us, "I'm not a perfect team member. I have strong opinions and am sometimes inflexible. But I came to value the work of teams. In the past, I was more in control. Working on a team is different. But I learned that I liked working on a team better than working alone." Each of the other members of Bruce's group had "a passion for doing things right" and was inspired by the goal of building a high-quality product for the union. "We'd get into heated discussions about even trivial things. In the end though, we were better off because of it."

This experience encouraged Bruce to move toward his Potential in two ways—the focus of his career and how he conducted himself. He told us that "I'm not always right and I need to seek out other viewpoints. I learned to value other views and listen to them much better than before." As a result of this experience and a subsequent project, Bruce got seriously interested in groups and what makes them work. A career shift was the eventual result: "I started working with teams on more projects and eventually made my way into doing full-time organization development work for the company."

Bruce's experience enabled him to see his own strengths and challenges and it pushed him into a different way of working. As it did so, it reinforced his Acceptance of himself and launched his Potential, which included new behaviors and a different professional path. Chapter Four addresses Acceptance and Potential in more detail.

Group–Bond and Purpose

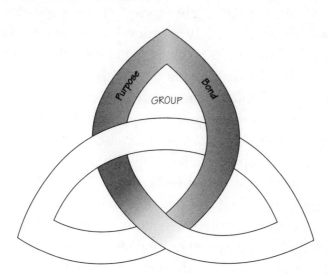

Most of us—hermits aside—want to live, work, and play in communities where our current and future selves are valued and supported. We bring our individual needs for Acceptance and Potential to a group where we meet others who bring those same longings. The group's declared Purpose creates the context for the relationships that develop as members of the group Bond with each other. The interplay between Bond and Purpose, in turn, encourages members' self-Acceptance and Potential. Let us offer some definitions:

- Bond: Our shared sense of identity and belonging
- Purpose: The reason we come together

Members show up hoping for a group to meet their needs to connect with others in a meaningful way. And so it is that the group offers a home—a place to be known and others to be known with. A place to be accepted, respected, and valued by others. A place that feels safe to contribute and discover. This intangible sense of "being on the same team"—of belonging—is what Bond is about. As bonded members join to pursue a common Purpose, they commit to something larger than themselves and their connection with one another. Through Purpose, they focus their attention, energy, skills, and communication—all within the context of a common compelling and unifying cause.

As with Acceptance and Potential, there is a creative and self-reinforcing dynamic between Bond and Purpose. Working together for a mutual Purpose allows members to get to know each other, thereby building their Bond. Increased appreciation for one another enables more concerted work toward Purpose. Creative thinking, collaboration, and commitment are common outgrowths of this interplay. Consider the following example of a group experience in which Bond and Purpose are particularly noticeable.

An International Donor's Circle

Allan sums up his group experience in this way: "This is the highest-performing team I've ever worked with." Which is saying something, given his forty-plus years of working in higher education, mental health services, and corporations in three different industries. Seven years ago, Allan was one of a small group of people who chose a positive, personal response to the September 11 attacks. They formed a donor's circle focused on small international development projects, making grants to people who might not otherwise have access to such funds. Examples include projects related to clean water, at-risk youth, small production agriculture, and preschool education in Asia, Latin America, or Africa. Members contribute $2,500 or $1,000 annually. They solicit proposals, recommend grantees, and then monitor the progress of the projects they fund—sometimes by visiting the projects. In 2002, they began with six members who granted $16,000 to three projects in one region of the world. At the end of 2008, there were forty-seven members funding twenty proposals amounting to $103,000 in three regions. Their contributions since 2002 exceed $250,000.

Sydney, a former scientist, joined the circle in 2006, not long after her retirement; she now finds herself the education chairperson and vice-president of the board. She sees the circle's Purpose as "a magnetic pull that brings us all together." When asked if she has been changed by the experience, her response was a resounding "Absolutely! I now spend twenty hours a week as a volunteer, have an incredible network of friends, and my worldview has expanded immeasurably."

Sydney's view is that the clear and powerful Purpose of the group creates a common framework in which decisions are made relatively easily, basically by consensus. A diverse membership includes strong and confident personalities, various ages and professional backgrounds, some who are wealthy, others who are not. Their meetings are characterized as "lively, with candor, and some joking and teasing. There's no complaining or criticism. It feels good—people are not uptight." Meetings typically begin with a potluck meal that encourages people to get to know each other better. And, of course, their various trips to remote parts of the world build strong connections with each other.

Allan reflects the group's Bond and Purpose saying, "There is great pride in what we are doing—that this is important and successful work. Not only in terms of our grantees and their work, but what we are each learning and how we engage more and more people locally in international philanthropy. This bonds us." He went on to say that "It's not that we've all become great friends. But there is genuine respect for what people bring and caring for each other. . . . Bond comes from the trust and respect that allows you to be yourself and be candid with others. They will listen and accept what you say. They will be candid with you. This is a very important part of the caring that goes on between people and what makes it possible to say things that feel risky."

Recently a conflict developed between a demanding founding member and someone new. Straight feedback, sensitively delivered, helped diffuse the conflict. Allan observed that when conflicts occur, "we communicate our way through to the other side." All members are drawn to the group's compelling Purpose; this makes it possible for them to "work things out and find a respectful compromise" rather than perpetuating conflicts or ending up in a situation where someone decides to leave the circle because of a disagreement.

Back and forth, Bond and Purpose reinforce one another, and in doing so, also make space for members to meet more self-oriented needs for Acceptance and Potential. Chapter Five addresses Bond and Purpose in more detail.

World-Reality and Impact

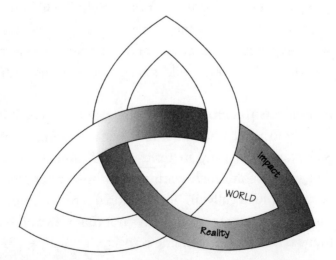

Depending on a group's Purpose, its "world" will vary. By this term, we mean the immediate setting that is most relevant to the group. This portion of the world may be as large as a corporation, an elementary school, a marketplace, a congregation, a city, a political constituency, or a family. Whatever it is, a group needs to understand its world in order to make a difference in it. The world Group Needs we each bring to groups are

- Reality: Understanding and accepting the world as it is and how it affects us
- Impact: Our intention to make a difference and our readiness to act

We are wired to survive; understanding our Reality is essential to that. As a species, our advancement has depended on being alert to the world around us. For groups to successfully fulfill their Purposes, members must demonstrate similar alertness; they need to see and accept the challenges and opportunities in front of them. When group members acknowledge Reality—rather than deny it—they increase the possibility of success.

Impact is about making a difference; it's about people coming together to make change for the better, moving their world a notch toward what they think that world ought to be. The creative dynamic between Reality and Impact can be highly pragmatic: when group members accept their Reality, they expand the possibility of Impact. This acceptance informs their strategies and actions. Or, perhaps more optimistically, with this understanding they can intentionally choose not to be limited by the real-world circumstances they face. Here's a story that illustrates these two Group Needs.

Saving $8.8 Million

Bob's employer manufactured, sold, and repaired sophisticated measurement instruments in the United States and overseas. In 2004, he faced an uncomfortable Reality: company cost reductions moved him from being a highly successful manufacturing manager to being an individual contributor. The reassignment saved his job but left him with no group to lead. And the company was seeking still greater cost reductions. Bob was assigned to the outsourcing team, a group of peers without a designated leader, charged with developing a new outsourcing strategy that would continue to produce savings. His new coworkers included three engineers, a purchasing expert, and a finance person.

The Impact of this outsourcing team has been very impressive. Their goal was to save $2 million in 2004; they saved $2.3 million. In 2005, they saved an additional $2.5 million, won the company's Innovation Award, and Bob was made manager of the group. By 2006, they had reduced costs over $2 million each year, for a total savings of $8.8 million. And how did they do it? They partnered with a U.S. vendor that could perform work that had previously been sent to one of the company's facilities in Malaysia. Partnering with this vendor achieved great savings and brought work and jobs back to the United States. It also required close cooperation between this new outside vendor and one factory.

A new Reality came as a consequence of work with the vendor: people in one factory—where Bob had formerly managed 200 people—were afraid the outsourcing team's work would lead to job loss. This plant had had multiple rounds of lay-offs over two years, and workers were concerned their jobs could go elsewhere. The outsourcing team was the bridge between the factory and the vendor; it became the target of factory workers' fears. For the outsourcing to be successful, vendor employees needed to learn to work with the instruments—and they needed to learn those skills from factory workers. The cooperation of plant workers was essential.

The team gathered for a day-long retreat, with a "pretty clear understanding of our purpose and the world we were operating in—how much we needed to save without taking a hit on any of the other business metrics." Bob recalls that "We set about learning each others' expertise and style, which turned out to be nicely complementary. And we realized we really needed each other's help." They redefined their roles and how they would work together. Every member took on a unique role based on his expertise and experience; a new sense of team cooperation emerged. Their collaborative plan was based on their shared assessment of Reality; collectively facing their challenges pulled the team together.

After the retreat, the finance person facilitated meetings; the purchasing person acted as an account manager with the vendor. The engineers figured out the process and cost of delivery issues. Because of Bob's experience in the plant where the fears had surfaced, he knew how to secure cooperation between plant employees and the vendor: managers would talk with each of the affected plant employees about the assignments they would move to when the current work was outsourced. Communication within the outsourcing team became relatively easy. As Bob commented, "It was hard to hide in a group of six. If people were holding back, they would be drawn out." They generally made their decisions by consensus but in certain cases deferred to the expertise of others.

Looking at the Impact of their work, Bob reflected on both the tangible and intangible results of the group's work. "At the start, there was no sense of 'we.'" But as the work evolved, "It was an amazing experience. It was an opportunity to solve a problem, to do something others thought was too hard to do, and to work with other competent people—on a project where we each could win!"

Let's look at the Group Needs model again, considering how each of the three loops is present in the Outsourcing Team's experience.

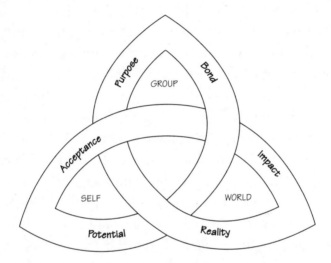

Without an understanding of the challenges (Reality) they faced, the Outsourcing Team could not have met and surpassed the expectations set for them (Impact). Confident team members (Acceptance) brought the necessary and complementary talents to their common goal (Purpose). They paid attention to how they worked together and supported each other's success (Bond), which reinforced their collective ability to have Impact. At least four of the group members expanded their skills in team building, influencing, or organizing in ways that prepared them for future roles (Potential). See Chapter Six for more detail on Reality and Impact.

When so many of group experiences are ordinary, people delight when a group stands out as unusual and positive—

groups like those Bruce, Bob, Allan, and Sydney experienced. In all sixty stories in our field study, at least three Group Needs were met. In fact, in the vast majority of cases, at least five of the six Group Needs were met. No wonder people could vividly recall those transforming groups!

Chapter Two discussed the eight indicators you are likely to see at work in extraordinary groups. And why do those indicators stand out? Because they meet the needs people bring to groups. And how do people feel when that happens? That's where we go next as we explore the feelings that come when Group Needs are met and transformation occurs.

At the Heart of Transformation

With the overview of the six Group Needs in place, we now describe what we mean by transformation and how it happens in groups. Among the questions asked in our interviews were these two: How were you changed by this experience? And What words would you use to describe this powerful experience? We collected literally hundreds of responses, studied them for patterns, and came to the conclusions we review in the rest of this chapter. Let's begin with a definition and elaborate on it with stories from earlier in the chapter:

> *Transformation* is a fundamental shift in individual perceptions that accelerates behavior change and personal vitality.

"A Fundamental Shift." We are not talking incremental change; we are not talking linear, logical movement. We are talking "the earth moved," "our bearings have shifted," "I now see it differently." This shift can be so subtle as to seem

small from an outside perspective, but the internal personal experience is profound.

"In Individual Perceptions." When perceptions shift at a fundamental level, the way an individual sees is altered; he has a new lens through which to view his world. For example, Bruce shifted from preferring to be an individual contributor to someone who wanted to work in teams. Allan shifted toward a more realistic view of the complex issues related to giving money internationally; he became more respectful of grantees and humble about his own circumstances. Sydney shifted the way she sets her priorities for her time and money. Bob learned the value of a "leaderless" group and how he could contribute to the group as a member and not the leader.

"That Accelerates Behavior Change." Individuals find themselves acting to support their new view of the world. They scramble to take advantage of it; they rededicate themselves, often giving more of themselves, working harder, longer, and differently with renewed purpose. Bruce began to listen more. Allan became more willing to compromise. Sydney convinced her family members to give donations to work in Kenya rather than holiday gifts to one another. Bob practiced being a team member, rather than a take-charge leader.

"And Personal Vitality." Because of the shift in perception, the individual feels more alive, more committed, connected, and contributing. That feeling is contagious within a group of individuals, transformed or not. The expression of alive feelings among people is often the first indicator that something transformative has occurred. Bruce

took away the sense that teaming with each other could be more fun, with more laughing, than he had ever imagined. Allan has seen that his work with the donors' circle "brings forth my best self." Sydney awakens eager to turn on her computer to see the news from those she has met around the world. Bob understands that his experience moved him from proposing teamwork—as he did when he managed manufacturing groups—to living it, now knowing "this stuff really works!"

Four Feelings at the Heart of Transformation

Those interviewees who felt they were transformed as defined in this chapter all experienced a similar set of four feelings. These four feelings fit with both individual and group transformative experiences, whether those of corporate planners, canoe trippers, ball players, software engineers, soldiers, college professors, or motorcyclists. All readily recognize these feelings. As varied as their purposes and uniforms, tools and contexts might be, this diverse array of people shared the same satisfaction. The feelings resulting from meeting their needs would show in their affirmative responses to these four questions:

- Did this experience *energize* you? Yes!
- Did you feel more deeply *connected* to your group or the world around you? Yes!
- Did you feel more *hopeful* about yourself, your group, or the world around you? Yes!
- Did you feel *changed* by this experience? Yes!

Four yeses point toward a transforming experience, as seen in this chapter's three stories. And when those affirmative answers are widely and enthusiastically expressed across a group, a transformative experience for many has probably occurred. Look for comments like, "What an exciting group! . . . I love our meetings! . . . You guys are great! . . . Look at what we've been able to accomplish!" If these questions and answers seem far removed from what your group might currently express, that could be a rough calculation of your distance from a transformative experience. Let's consider each of these four key feelings.

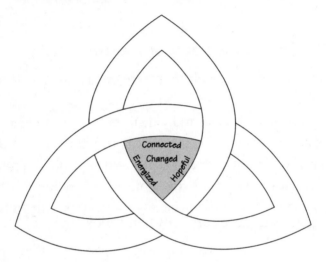

Energized! A sense of vitality increases as members engage with the group and the world. The sixty people we interviewed were all energized by recalling their experiences —even the one who didn't think he had been changed by the experience, or the four whose groups fell short of their desired Impact. These people became animated as they told their stories; they loved recreating the experience for us and for themselves. Just listening to them mirrored the high engagement and total investment that they experienced at the time. As you watch your groups, this energy will show as the group interacts; you will notice how alive the group is from one moment to the next; members will notice their vitality as it is sparked or dampened in group exchange. Vitality becomes a common, quick measure of what is happening, as in, "Does this have life for us?" Or "What about this project brings energy to you?"

Connected! People are often surprised at how connected they feel with their group. They were typically astounded by their feelings of being tightly bonded with other group members who at the beginning seemed so different from themselves. For some, it was the most accepting group they had ever been part of. They were uniquely, even permanently joined. It was not uncommon that people who told us about twenty-year-old experiences could put us immediately in touch with others who had been in the group. We heard these comments about the connections people felt with one another: "We bonded for life." "There was an informal heart-and-soul group made up of those who were willing to do whatever was necessary." "When I took this job, I thought I'd only be here for two years. The team and mission have kept me here for seven." Members personally connect to each other, to the group itself, to its Purpose, and to the difference they make together.

Hopeful! As people told their stories, we could hear the hope implied in all that the group did as it moved toward creating a better product, place, or world. Because of what their groups did and because they were part of it, people leaned toward the future with a more optimistic outlook. They held the sense that they were making a difference on something important. Hopefulness is further fed by the fact a uniquely capable group is doing this together. If there were more groups like this in the world, there would be less to worry about! Some examples of what we heard: "Each of us represented different nationalities. Somehow we met in the universe with different values and we discovered that we speak the same language and have so much in common!" "There are no boundaries for what we can do. We can be in a completely free creation mode." "I have experienced the power of our ability to positively influence kids who could go either way. They are ready and willing when we give them the skills. We see it in front of our eyes. It's quite incredible!" "I can help others by helping myself and utilizing all of my skills. This has made me feel relevant and useful. Together we have a sense of how it can be different." And the hope they have created here is contagious. It tells them what just might be possible in other realms of their lives.

Changed! All but one person we interviewed affirmed that they saw changes in themselves that could be tied directly to the group they told us about. For some, the change was dramatic and noticeable. For example: "It's made my life livable." For others, the change was more subtle: "It confirmed what I have believed for some time." Some saw immediate impact: "I immediately knew that I was not alone. I had a global network of people I could call at any time—no matter what." Others sensed the power of the experience over time: "The work didn't seem like work anymore. My whole way of thinking about my work changed. I wanted to be the Charlie Parker of computer skills training. I wanted it to be like jazz—a bunch of really talented people working in chaos to make something beautiful." Each quote is testimony to how things will never be quite the same again.

To summarize, when you feel energized, connected, hopeful, and changed, you've probably had a transformative experience. When you ask others in your group about how they feel, and their responses fit with these four feelings, your group has probably been through something transforming and terrific together! All of this comes together visually in this illustration.

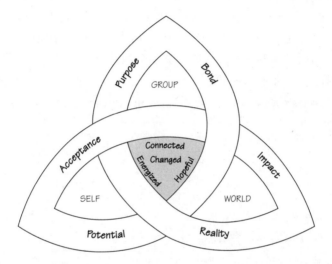

How Transformation Happens in a Group

In a group, how to we get to these four feelings? First, by attending to the six Group Needs: Acceptance and Potential, Bond and Purpose, Reality and Impact. People will feel energized, connected, hopeful, and changed as their Group Needs are met. Second, by behaving in ways that demonstrate the eight indicators highlighted in Chapter Two. If you were sitting in the back of the room watching an extraordinary and transforming group, you'd see signs of a compelling purpose, shared leadership, just-enough-structure, embracing differences, full engagement, unexpected learning, strong relationships, and great results. Such actions also trigger feelings of being energized, connected, hopeful and changed. Let's look more concretely at how this happens.

Transformation Is a Heart-Felt Experience

We have described the six Group Needs as *instinctive* or *intuitive* or *unconscious*. When two or more of those needs are met, the impact is felt within nonrational, emotional, very human territory. As we go about our daily routines, we humans operate simultaneously on at least two tracks. Think of them as the "head" and the "heart." Each is associated with elements that shape how we experience life, the meaning we take from it, and the behaviors we choose. For example, consider this table:

Head	Facts	Logic	Analysis	Knowing	Practical	Transition
Heart	Emotions	Intuition	Meaning	Sensing	Passionate	Transformation

Especially at work, the head gets lots of attention. Think of job descriptions, plans, roles, decisions, data reports, metrics, and organizational charts. All are useful in joining people for accomplishment. And the head is just part of the person. When people in our field study used short phrases to describe their transformative experiences, passion, emotion, and enthusiasm were the pattern. The enthusiasm people express describing their extraordinary groups told us that to understand transformation, we needed to explore terrain beyond analysis and logic, beyond the head and into the heart.

Transformation Happens to One Person at a Time

Our experience and our field study reinforce that transformation happens first as a unique experience for the individual. It happens one person at a time and it happens differently for each person—though the expression of that experience will have much in common with the expressions of others.

Someone can consciously expose a group to experiences that make transformation more likely, but in the end each member will experience transformation in a private and personal way.

Transformation Seldom Happens Simultaneously for an Entire Group

When this group-shift does happen, the effect is electric. What happens for one group member resonates with others, making a similar reaction more likely. Members feed on each other's energy, caught up in what is happening around them. Our guidance on how to meet Group Needs can make this more likely, but group transformation isn't delivered through linear steps or a formula. You can make it more likely, but in the end you must yield to forces in the moment, to chance, to intuition. These are the moments that people describe as "magical."

Transformation Is Personal and Not Guaranteed

There is no way to guarantee transformation. We wish there were. But transformation is simply too private and subjective a process to be controlled or predicted by another person. Transformation often happens quietly without a lot of fanfare or external recognition—even when it turns out to be tremendously significant. For the most part, the powerful shift of perspective is recognized only after it happens. Similarly, the power of the shift cannot be judged by anyone else. We can only make these judgments for ourselves.

Transformation Can Be Encouraged

We are convinced that you can significantly increase the likelihood of individual and group transformation. In story after story, we heard of multiple Group Needs being met in experiences that people saw as amazing. Group members, leaders, and facilitators behaved in ways that fit with creating a transformed group. Consider what you could do to help one of your groups move from ordinary to extraordinary. What might you do or say that would cause others—or yourself—to feel energized, connected, hopeful, and changed?

Parts Two and Three of this book will help you think more about this.

Part Two

UNDERSTANDING THE GROUP NEEDS MODEL

Part One introduced the Group Needs model; Part Two helps you understand it more deeply and begin to apply its components. Chapters Four, Five, and Six expand on the Self, Group, and World loops of the model, one loop per chapter. They offer more detail about the six Group Needs and what you can do to gain greater understanding of them. Stories illustrate the paired Group Needs in each loop; application guidance comes in the form of reflection questions to ask of yourself and actions you might take, usually with your groups. Chapter Seven explores what happens at the center of the knot as the six Group Needs overlap and result in powerful and transformative experiences.

If you want to push further into the application of the Group Needs model, refer to Appendix A for a set of exercises that will help you put into practice the ideas offered in Part Two.

4

GROWING TOWARD
YOUR POTENTIAL

Jeanette had little idea of what was ahead of her when she agreed to help design a community college course on product life cycle management. In her late fifties and a small business owner, Jeanette had significant expertise in product life cycles, lean manufacturing processes, and instructional design. As she began work on the project, she discovered that she was in brand new territory—in several ways. The audience for the course was a group she had never designed for: technicians who repair and maintain things made of composite materials, for example, boats and airplanes. In fact, Jeanette had never even heard of composite materials. In addition, the course would be taught online, and she had never before developed an online course. And she had never met the man she was to collaborate with, who lived ninety miles away; this meant that most of their work would be done at a distance rather than face to face. Again—not what she was used to.

From March through May, Jeanette worked closely with her new colleague, Ed, relying on phone, the Internet, and shared software that enabled them to see and work on the same documents on their respective computers. In fact, in the three intense months of their work, they probably spent less than ten hours together in the same location; typically that would happen when they met with Mary Kay, the program administrator at the college. Jeanette quickly saw that Ed was an effective team player; they both found ways to contribute their different expertise: "I looked at how to introduce this material, then provided content on lean manufacturing and Six Sigma. Ed looked at it as an engineer, bringing computer-assisted design skills and other tools."

From Jeanette's view, this was an important project and very motivating. It was a chance "to help create a wonderful product for the students that they could take anywhere in the world." Commenting on the trio they formed with Mary Kay, she observed that "the right people got pulled in with the right skills at the right time. Each came with their own strengths and we complemented each other." In addition to their different backgrounds, they had very different styles of working and communicating. Such differences, which could have been challenging, were not—thanks to their well-developed people-skills, genuine respect for one another's skill sets, and joint commitment to the project and its deadlines.

Working on the project every day, Jeanette and Ed developed a plan of what needed to be done and who would take the lead on which portion of the work. Then came their individual work: Ed focusing on the computer-assisted design components, Jeanette concentrating on the more conceptual content. They'd talk on the phone and work online, showing each other their individual work and asking, "Does this work for you?" Back and forth, making their way through the design, deciding important issues together, serving as sounding-boards for each other, and figuring out what needed to be done next and who would do it. Then following through. Looking back, Jeanette says "I suppose we had some 'storming' with each other, but I can't remember it. Maybe we just didn't have the time for that."

When reflecting on the transformative impact of this project, she was easily able to see that "It helped my self esteem. This was very life affirming. It reminded me that 'I can do this!'" She added, "It's very easy to start feeling useless in your late fifties. Thanks to this project, I feel more confident. It's expanded my personal and professional network. And learning the new hybrid technology for instructional design was wonderful. I learned I want to stay on top of technology and not lose my skills! This was a synergistic breakthrough for me."

Stories like Jeanette's reflect the fact that the whole panoply of human interaction—starting with two individuals and expanding outward to a group, an organization, a society, a state, a world—is a fractal-like edifice built upon the single and significant individual. As a maple leaf offers the outlines of the maple tree, so the individual offers the outlines of the group, and the group of the organization, and so on. The individual is always there, embedded in more and more complex dynamics. This truth has profound implications for groups and for our model. Strong groups grow from strong individuals, and that is what this chapter focuses on: the core strength of an individual that comes from self-Acceptance and the drive to develop one's Potential.

Overview of Acceptance and Potential

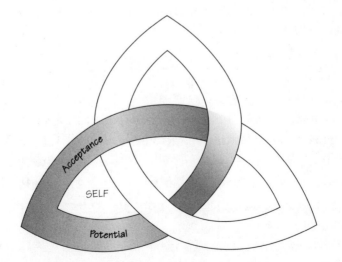

As the Group Needs model shows, Acceptance and Potential are two parts of the Self loop. The most personal of the six Group Needs, we humans work to satisfy them whether we are in a group or not. They pertain to the universal self—elements that each of us knows internally and privately. Taken together they help us be strong. Because they are so personal, we'd like to write about them, at least briefly, in the first person—from the "I" position. Consider reading the next few paragraphs out loud so that you can hear these words more personally, as statements about yourself. As you take in our thoughts, consider whether our statements are true for you and how they are reflected in Jeanette's story.

Acceptance is about my strengths and weaknesses and my ability to observe myself. At a deeper level, this is about my identity, knowing who I am and embracing myself as I am. This need continues throughout my life and is regularly challenged by new circumstances. When I am more accepting of who I am, I move from my center with more confidence into the future. Paired with the need for Acceptance is the need to experience Potential. My Potential is the "me" I long to become and my willingness to reshape myself toward that vision. The need to do so stems from my internal knowledge that I could be different, I could be more. But how? This growing of myself requires internal searching, risking, and acting to test my learning self out in the world.

Because strong groups grow from strong individuals, Acceptance and Potential are also powerful Group Needs; they influence the way in which we Bond with others around a group Purpose so that we can take in the Reality of our group's circumstances in order to collectively make an Impact.

Acceptance: Knowing and Appreciating Ourselves for Who We Are

Picture an individual alone, not engaged in a group at the moment. That person's first need is to accept himself by knowing and appreciating himself for who he is. This need is reflected in three statements:

- I know who I am and what I bring, strengths and limitations
- I can express who I am to myself and others
- I accept myself for who I am right now

Of course, that person has more Group Needs—needs we will explore in coming chapters—but for the moment we are focused on a core need that provides the foundation for others to come. Self-Acceptance is the basis for confidence and personal power. When an individual knows his starting point, he can better travel the road ahead. As we elaborate on these three statements, notice how they fit with you and your personal needs and how they surfaced in Jeanette's story.

I Know Who I Am and What I Bring, Strengths and Limitations

Underlying our success in some groups, undermining our success in others, is our knowledge of ourselves. And the accuracy of it. The résumé information is one thing; talents are another. Yes, it's hard to know what you bring to the party if you've never been to this party before—but that's exactly what you are called upon to do. For your own sake, you need to know what you are pretty good at, not so good at, and outstandingly good at! Knowing who you are gives you a starting position for your engagement with others. Self-knowledge is the first step toward self-Acceptance and expression.

I Can Express Who I Am to Myself and Others

When you join a group, you need enough clarity about yourself so that you can speak about yourself to others. The more clarity you have, the more articulate you are likely to be. The process of getting to know yourself—and learning to express who you are—comes from the capacity to be self-reflective. Personal reflections cause you to step back from yourself and become aware of what you are thinking, feeling, and doing. These awareness-building observations often translate into self-talk—internal reflections and messages that, for some, can take on a conversational quality. It is much easier to be articulate about yourself to others if you have given yourself the gift of self-reflection, self-observation, or self-talk that is both positive and accurate.

I Accept Myself for Who I Am Right Now

Self-Acceptance goes beyond just knowing and expressing yourself; it also includes being comfortable in doing so. An ease with yourself in the present is one reflection of Acceptance. Not who you might be in the future—but comfort in and appreciation of who you really are right now. For many of us, that is a recurring challenge: to embrace our whole selves: talents, style, warts, strengths, blemishes, weaknesses—the whole works—right now. Personal growth sprouts more readily in the soil of self-Acceptance than on the rocks of self-condemnation. Many of us have made it a long way on self-criticism, but that is an overused strategy;

it should yield to a more positive, self-affirming alternative. Often, what we cannot accept in ourselves, we cannot accept in others. The ability to accept ourselves leads to our ability to accept others.

The success of your work in groups is highly dependent on the work you have done within yourself. For example, take full engagement, which we discussed in Chapter Two. That wonderful ability to be fully present in a group, bringing ideas, questions, and opinions—to speak without hesitation. Where does that behavior come from? In large part, from being able to affirm the three statements above. Those self-aware statements give individuals the confidence to speak and to listen. Test those statements on yourself. And test the opposite. Most of us know also know the times when we could not affirm those three statements, when we felt lost, less able to express or accept who we were in the moment. These heavy negative feelings offer sad confirmation that something important is missing, that our longing to be ourselves is not being met.

Potential: Sensing and Growing into Our Fuller and Better Selves

In describing the need to accept oneself, we dropped a few clues about the second personal and Group Need, realizing one's Potential. Three statements combine to express that second need.

- I sense that I could be more
- I am drawn to the possibilities
- I want to learn and grow

Continue to think about Jeanette—and yourself—as you read more about these statements.

I Sense That I Could Be More

You watch your life unfold. You cannot help but compare today to yesterday, noting what happened and what allowed it to be. As you learn from your recent history, you also imagine tomorrow. You know that you can influence the future and sense your potential to do so. You know you do not have to be today what you have always been, that you are far from finished, that you could be more tomorrow than you are today.

I Am Drawn to the Possibilities

Like most others, you probably hunger for wholeness. You want to and lean toward becoming your very best self. You want to bring your Potential to life, to activate your better self in the world. Individuals vary in that motive, but we each know about that inclination within ourselves; we each decide how to act on it. Sometimes, busyness crowds out our view of the possibilities, but they are still there. This wonderful predisposition to move toward your Potential provides a key motivational force within transformed groups.

I Want to Learn and Grow

As a most vulnerable species, we have had to learn to survive. We humans have excelled at learning and have the cerebral cortex to prove it. In the more modern world, many of us have the freedom to look beyond survival and learn in areas that could help us thrive. Knowing who we are now and anticipating what we might become defines a space to be filled with learning. We must grow in order to move from who we are now to what we want to become. An open stance toward learning and a spirit of discovery will serve you well in a world that seems determined to distract you. If you want to create fantastic groups, know that most people long to discover more about themselves, to act on their possibilities, and to learn in service of their Potential.

This well of Potential has an unplumbed depth. From an early age, we declare what we want to be when we grow up. And we ask our children what they want to be. We ask adults the question less often as they grow into their work, but they hold the question within them. It does not take long over coffee or a beer to get most of us to speak to what we could be, our possibilities. And not just work possibilities, but life possibilities. Sometimes it's as concrete as a residence, a vacation, a position, or a degree; often it's as vague as a dream of contribution, making a difference, leaving a legacy. In all but the most discouraged, these aspirations suggest what could really motivate this person. These aspirations are the foundation of change. Whether we set about changing ourselves or our group or our world, the aspiration to become more will pull us forward. What a different motivational force this is than just fixing what's wrong! Potential is not about fixing; it is about fulfilling. And this is where we must go if we are to grow and involve others in growing.

The Creative Dynamic Between Acceptance and Potential

Sense the creative dynamic between Acceptance and Potential within yourself. As you can see in the following table, these two needs inform each other. On the one side, you embrace who you are; on the other side, you reach out for more. The space between those two sides creates a dynamic that can aid your fulfillment—just as it did for Jeanette.

The Creative Dynamic of Acceptance and Potential

Acceptance: Knowing and Appreciating Myself for Who I Am.	*The Creative Dynamic* ↔	*Potential*: Sensing and Growing into My Fuller/Better Self.
I accept myself for who I am right now	↔	I sense that I could be more
I know who I am and what I bring	↔	I am drawn to my possibilities
I can express who I am to myself and others	↔	I want to learn and grow

She accepted the assignment to help create the new college course because she knew that her current capabilities would enable her to be up to the task. When she discovered that this experience would be filled with so many new elements, the clarity and confidence created by her self-Acceptance enabled her to move into the unknown as a learner. Through her partnership with Ed, she built new skills and mastered new content. The result was an enhanced self-esteem and excitement about what she is now prepared to bring to her next assignment.

Embracing Acceptance and Potential simultaneously gives you a third view; you are stretched to consider, How do I do all of this at once? Present and future, Reality and possibility, yin and yang may be awakened within you. Living in the whole loop defined by these two paired Group Needs stirs you when you seek to fulfill both. Your motivation is larger than what comes from considering one side of the loop or the other. Words within this fertile space include knowledge, expression, acceptance, motivation, potential, anticipation, comfort, learning, risk, power, clarity, excitement—words that fit with our interviews with members of extraordinary groups.

Think about professional sports teams playing to win within the boundaries of its game. As spectators, we see from their struggle that this game is important. After the game, ask individuals why they play and you will hear an array of responses that point to important motivations that lie below the surface: loving the game, being paid big bucks, gaining recognition, serving God, achieving fairness and equality, being a model for kids, providing for family, having fun, using a unique talent, loving to win, achieving personal best. These various motives emerge when individual players go through the thinking discussed in this chapter. When each player knows who she is and what she wants, each can more powerfully join with the other members to form a team—and be ready to fulfill the team's purpose: winning the game. Without the individual clarity that comes from the interplay between Acceptance and Potential, the team will struggle to find its center. And so it is with the rest of us too. Know who you are, what you bring, and what you aspire to. This awareness empowers you and you will empower your group.

Guidance: Ways to Meet the Needs of Acceptance and Potential

Because self-Acceptance and Potential are uniquely personal among the six Group Needs, our guidance is focused on you and you alone. Other loops of the model, in the next two chapters, will help you think about yourself in relation to your groups and the world. But here, we consider you as an individual to build the awareness and strength you bring to your groups. Four suggestions focus on your self-Acceptance and Potential:

- Learn about yourself and your Potential
- Accept yourself in order to accept others

- Understand and apply your strengths
- Learn in order to live more fully

The remainder of this chapter builds on these suggestions with questions that ask you to reflect on the ideas we've presented. Those questions are followed by sample actions— perhaps useful as you prepare yourself to be an even more effective person and group member. You will find us using this same pattern in most of the remaining chapters: content followed by questions for you and actions for you with your group. And if you want to learn even more, turn to Appendix A; you'll find exercises that build nicely on this chapter and the next two.

Now move ahead with this chapter with a journal in hand. Reflect on yourself as you read, take a few notes, and consider possible actions that acknowledge where you are today (Acceptance) and move you toward where you would like to be tomorrow (Potential).

Learn About Yourself and Your Potential

In the ebb and flow of good times and harder times, our experience in groups provides us with the regular and constant opportunity to reflect on ourselves, to accept who we have become so far, and to discover our Potential.

Reflection Questions for You. Use the Group Needs model to more deeply understand yourself and how you engage with groups of friends, coworkers, neighbors, and family members. This internal work begins before you show up with the group. You do not have to wait until the next meeting to discover more about yourself. The upcoming questions relate to your need to know yourself as you are now and how you might be within your Potential. Answer them and your needs will move into sharper focus:

- How would you describe yourself in twenty-five words or less?
- How would others describe you?
- How much do you prefer working with others versus working alone?
- What are the advantages to you of the ways you prefer to work?
- When you think about your future, how is it similar to or different from what you are doing today?
- Where do you get your inspiration? Where does it lead you?

Notice how easy or difficult it was to answer these questions. Your readiness to answer suggests something about how alive these questions are in your life. Quick, lengthy, deep responses suggest the questions are more alive for you, that you are more aware of who you are and what you want to become. If the questions lead you to unfamiliar ground and your responses are slower in coming, perhaps that indicates a fruitful place for your continuing reflection. The crux of the Self loop of our model is that self-awareness leads to personal power, and in our minds, awareness includes the ability to express your observations of yourself. Your personal Group Needs of Acceptance and Potential stand behind each of these questions and your answers.

Sample Actions for You. Here you'll find a set of suggestions for actions you can take to learn more about yourself and your Potential.

- Think about the qualities you bring to groups. Don't think about this deeply; answer off the top of your head—much as you might if a friend were to ask you. Write down your main thoughts. Consider how well these thoughts represent you, and your comfort with your answers.

- Reflect on one group that is particularly important to you. Make notes to yourself on these questions: What have you learned from participating in this group? How has this learning been important for you? Of the six Group Needs, which does this group meet for you? Which of your Group Needs are regularly frustrated in this group?

- After reviewing the explanation of the Self loop early in this chapter, note what you could do to better meet your Group Needs of Acceptance and Potential in the group you just wrote about. Write actions you might take.

Accept Yourself in Order to Accept Others

We are all works in progress, with flairs and flaws, strengths and limitations. Others can help us become more accepting of ourselves when they acknowledge our contributions. But let's face it, many of us are regularly frustrated in our accomplishments and are critical of ourselves as a result. Those frustrations are so widely felt as to suggest they are a natural part of life. When we live with this as a life truth, it suggests that we might be well served by being more accepting and less critical of ourselves. That in turn will lead to us being more accepting of others. We cannot appreciate in others what we are critical of in ourselves. These thoughts are central to the following questions and actions.

Reflection Questions for You. Knowing yourself is empowering; these questions lead to answers that strengthen you.

- What do you regularly appreciate about yourself? What characteristics? Talents? Idiosyncrasies?
- What do you regularly have a hard time accepting in yourself?
- How could you be more accepting of yourself as you are right now?
- How do your views on yourself affect your views of others? Cite examples.
- What are your thought patterns about others—in terms of your appreciation or criticism—while working with others in groups?
- What could you better appreciate about yourself that might lead to appreciation of others?

Sample Actions for You. These actions are especially valuable when attended to over time. Expect long-term results to come through that regular attention.

- Practice deeper appreciation of yourself. Make a list of what is wonderful about you. Notice how you feel about that one-sided list. Feelings of embarrassment or unworthiness suggest you have more work to do.
- Note something about yourself that you routinely do not appreciate. Now, ask yourself how that behavior or characteristic serves you well in your life. There must be some reasons that you keep doing this.
- Engage a friend in talking about an aspect of your own behavior or personality that you regularly have difficulty

with. Ask your friend how he or she lives with this quality of yours—and how you might.

- When someone you know is deeply critical of himself in a way that negatively affects him, help him move toward a recognition of this as a common human condition and Acceptance of who he is right now—flaws and all. Do this by expressing your appreciation for the fine qualities he brings to your group, empathizing with him about the challenge of dealing with personal flaws, and recalling similar struggles with Acceptance in your own life.

Understand and Apply Your Strengths

Our interviews show that in extraordinary groups, people are respected as individuals and for their knowledge and skills. When they apply their talents to group Purpose, others value them and their strengths. This emphasis on strengths rather than flaws fuels a motivating climate of respect and appreciation. This positive mind-set encourages people to accept themselves, warts and all. Acceptance in the group is rooted in self-Acceptance by each individual.

Reflection Questions for You. Look into yourself for qualities that are important to you but seldom get expression.

- What talents do you regularly bring to your groups?
- How might you better bring your full self to those groups?
- How can you help others you work with recognize and utilize the talent you bring?
- What talents are you withholding that you truly believe would be useful?
- What could you do to gain greater Acceptance of your shortcomings along with your talents?

Sample Actions for You. To actively apply your strengths in one of your groups, you may need to let people know directly about your talents, knowledge or skills. You can also use your interactions with group members as a way to gain greater insight about your strengths.

- More frequently express what you can or would like to contribute. Do so with the spirit of making an offer rather than bragging.
- Think, speak, and act more in terms of how you can help, not how you cannot.
- When you are not getting the appreciation you need, ask for some feedback on what you have contributed and its impact.
- Ask others what they value that you contribute to groups. And ask what else you might do.
- Ask others which of your behaviors might detract from your own or group performance. Make a point of understanding them fully.

Learn in Order to Live More Fully

Early humans learned to adapt to survive, and we continue to do so today. We must learn in order to live our lives at a basic level. And we must learn in order to be fully alive and thrive: engaged, curious, imaginative, creative, risk-taking—and yet practical and grounded in Reality. We know from our sixty interviews about extraordinary groups that learning is pervasive. What is exciting to the group is rooted in the individual. With that in mind, the following questions and actions pursue your excitement.

Reflection Questions for You. At some level for all of us, work and life are joined—as these questions suggest. When you think of "work" include what you do in your volunteer life.

- What kinds of questions about work and life do you find yourself regularly intrigued by? Why?
- Who do you like to talk with about your questions? What do you find rewarding about those discussions?
- What kind of work do you like to do—to the point you would almost do it even if you were not paid?
- If you had the time and money to learn something brand new to you, what would it be?
- What is your reaction to the line of questioning we are pursuing here? Why?

Each of these questions attempts to move you beyond your regular experience in the direction of what your life might be if you learned more. The intent is not to create a plan as much as to become more aware of what excites you about learning and the directions your learning and your life might take, given the option.

Sample Actions for You. Practice seeing your work through the lens of your life—as these actions suggest.

- Describe a time in your life when you were excited about learning. Describe the circumstances that surrounded that great experience, all that allowed it to happen. Consider how that time compares to your present life and work, and what you could do about it.
- Make an intentionally ambitious, even unrealistic, list of what you would like to learn more about in your work, your community, your life.

- Volunteer for action that uses your existing skills and stretches you to learn new ones.

- Develop a plan for personal growth, including the steps you will take. Seek help from others along the way. Report to them on what you are doing.

- In one of your groups, express what you want to learn and why this is important to you.

This completes our exploration of Acceptance and Potential. We hope that our suggestions for questions to reflect upon and actions to take have given you some increased sense of your current and future self. Chapter Five moves you from the Self loop of our model into the Group loop and the needs for Bond and Purpose.

5

JOINING FOR PURPOSE

"Anything is possible!" Suzi took this life-changing mes-
sage away from her work on the 2008 presidential campaign.
A corporate marketing executive turned stay-at-home mom
with two young children, she went from having nothing to
do with politics to national involvement. In less than one
year. All of this started with one simple question: What else
can I do to help?

In Suzi's state, party caucuses select presidential candi-
dates. People in neighborhood precincts select delegates, who
attend a county caucus where delegates are chosen to go to
a state caucus, resulting in national delegates who go to the
party's national convention. Suzi attended her precinct caucus in February and at the close asked what else she could do
to help. Six months and three levels later, she found herself
at the national political convention. And she continued vol-
unteering right through election day.

The amazing group in Suzi's experience involved about
fourteen volunteers; sometimes more and sometimes fewer,
depending on the phase of the campaign. These people,
plus one paid staff member, showed up and worked tirelessly
between caucus rounds. Their Purpose grew as the process
unfolded. Initially they made sure pledged delegates showed
up at the next caucus. As the campaign and group matured,
they took on more responsibility. They assessed their candidate's vulnerability to other contenders; they assured a strong
presence at all events; they strategized to assure diversity of

selected delegates. They identified potential delegates who could use the title of "national delegate" to encourage new voters in the general election. As the weeks flew by, Suzi recalls that "we were beating the odds. We felt if we worked hard enough, we would make it happen!"

Geographically spread, members relied on technology to support their collaboration, which Suzi sees as a major strength of the group. They e-mailed, they texted; they relied on a campaign Web site and Google documents to provide them with guidance. "We were empowered to make a difference. We felt that everything we did would help to make a difference in the country and in the world." Everyone had a job to do; all were focused on getting their candidate elected. In addition to dealing with a strong opposing campaign, they were challenged to "stay in the loop with one another." Several times a week, conference calls allowed the group to discuss the more complex issues. They made very few Yes or No decisions. More often in their discussions someone would propose an idea or action and ask, What do you think? Each person involved was highly committed to getting their candidate elected. When tempers would flare and "things got heated, we would go back to that point and regroup."

Success depended on follow through. And people did. Collectively members seemed to have the right skills, "so that we could plug people in when we needed to" to get things done. Because of the trust in the group, people let others move ahead. This Bond developed quickly, primarily through the phone calls: "After just two weeks of working so intensely together, it felt like we had been doing this for much longer! Our energy got channeled so quickly! . . . With too much to do and operating in a dispersed way, we had to trust each other." When asked about bonding, she told us that "we all worked closely together through to the actual election, supporting each other's efforts"—whether working crowds at summer parades or ringing door-bells in neighborhoods. Understandably, there was an even tighter Bond among those who were delegates at the national convention.

Looking back on her extraordinary year, Suzi knows that her experience was transforming. "I volunteer a lot more now and am more locally aware." Now linked through a Google group to other national delegates, she knows that this difference in her life represents "a long-term change. It has changed me and my family. My six-year-old son tells people 'Mommy helped get the President elected' and my younger daughter went with me to knock on doors in Florida. My kids know that one individual can have a global impact." Suzi is clear: "For me this was life-changing."

Overview of Bond and Purpose

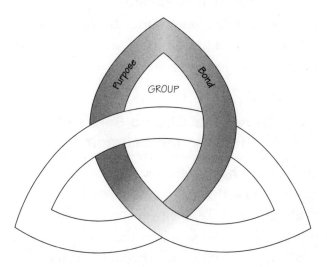

The last chapter highlighted our needs for Acceptance and Potential; as individuals, we bring these two needs when we join a group. This chapter addresses the two Group Needs we meet within a group: the Bond that holds the group together and the Purpose that the group commits to achieving. As with Acceptance and Potential, Bond and Purpose are linked; they represent the two sides of the Group loop in our model.

At work, home, and in the community, we live in small groups; we express ourselves through groups; we form our identities within groups; we appraise who we are by what happens to us in groups. And as we do all of this, we hone our skills, giving and receiving from these smallish groups of people who Bond together in Purpose. Bond and Purpose are inextricably linked. We find it hard to think about one without referring to the other. As in Suzi's campaign group, the shared passionate commitment to their Purpose fed the Bond between them. Their mutual trust and collective identity fueled the energy and drive that was needed to sustain them through countless phone calls, meeting after meeting, late nights, and early mornings.

We now consider Bond and Purpose in some depth. Then we offer guidance, reflections, and actions to meet your own Group Needs for Bond and Purpose, as well as support other group members in doing the same.

Bond: Our Shared Sense of Identity and Belonging

Groups provide the human contact we need: We "be-*long*" to a group. As we Bond with other members, we establish our shared sense of identity and belonging. This is where "Everybody knows your name," as they say on that old TV show, *Cheers*. At their best, groups enfold us, they love us for who we are, and they are protect us no matter what. We like groups small enough that we can know everyone and large enough to give us a sense of shared power. Whether a neighborhood or a social club, joining with others of like mind helps us feel safe.

Group bonds develop over time, seldom instantaneously. They are built from the continued contact of those involved. Members joined with Purpose in mind may be surprised to discover that somehow they have bonded along the way. Developing that Bond is like dipping a candle. The strength comes from reinforcing the connection, layer upon layer, time after time. Some groups discover they have a Bond even more important than their original Purpose. When group Bond is working, members are likely to agree, individually and collectively, with these statements:

- We know who we are together.
- We create a safe space for each other.
- We each play our parts.

Synergistically, each statement builds on the others. Here are some elaborations and connections. Think about Suzi's experience as you read ahead.

We Know Who We Are Together

Members joining a new group arrive with a sense of themselves and their futures—strongly or weakly formed. However we show up, we build from here. The previous chapter supports arriving more strongly, but whoever we are at this moment, we want to know each other and build our actions upon that. We need to know ourselves individually to help build our collective sense of our ourselves as a group. And our group is more than a collection of individual selves. The chemistry among us will give our group its own identity. As we join with others, we get to know each other in the context of our Purpose. An identity begins to form for the group that includes "who we are, what we are capable of, and how we do things here." These understandings help define the group. Extraordinary groups lay a foundation based upon getting to know one another because they know they will need to rely on each other soon.

We Create a Safe Place for Each Other

A group needs a place—even if it is in cyberspace. Members need a place to meet, where the individuals can become the group. And it must be safe enough to learn about the diverse talents, backgrounds, and perspectives available in the group. Safety within the group is important to risking together out in the world. We have enough to worry about "out there" as we pursue our Purpose. We don't want to complicate our work "in here" with murky dynamics, mistrust, and a energy-consuming internal process. What happens inside the group is predictable—in the best senses of that word. Even passionate disagreements can feel reassuring—when we expect them. Even expressing mistakes can feel good—if "that's the way we do things around here."

Members of extraordinary groups often develop a commitment to each other that is beyond reason. They can feel so close, so tight, as to feel even tribal. One interviewee spoke of being a "blood brother" with other team members! "Tribal" callsup from the past our more primitive notions of self, where we came from. We may have overlaid those ancient dynamics with more sophisticated twenty-first century forms, but they have not disappeared. The iPhones and Blackberries that connect us in the twenty-first century are often meeting ancient tribal needs.

We Each Play Our Part

Do not start looking for your script; it is much more intricate than that. Your group is a "play" in which you write your own role while others write theirs. And you do this simultaneously, all in search of your place in the group, a place that can continue to shift through time. As others redefine their parts, as circumstance changes the demands on the group, as group purpose shifts, as your life priorities change, all of this affects the part you play. In extraordinary groups, members know what to expect of each other. And they know that all of the parts are key to their success. They know who the strategist is. And the detail person. And the optimist. And the clown. And the action people, the cautious people, the reticent people, and who gets this group moving. They love seeing all this come together in ways unique to this one amazing group.

Our various parts are affected by having an explicit, declared Purpose but are not dependent on that; we gravitate toward our roles because of the talent we bring and want to contribute and because of how we want to grow into our Potential. While Bond is mostly about internal dynamics between members, Purpose links those members to the world outside the group.

Purpose: The Reason We Come Together

Just as we need to connect with others, we also long to be joined with others in shared Purpose—the reason we come together. We group to extend our reach and influence, or to do work, or to, as in Suzi's example, help get a particular candidate elected president. We come together in an effort that is larger than ourselves, where collective energy and capacity combine to achieve something that could or would never be done by individuals alone. At their best, groups know why they exist, where they are going, and their members are ready to give what is expected of them to fulfill the common Purpose.

We see two primary group purposes: (1) Purpose focused outward on change in the world outside the group. Groups in the workplace and community typically set out to affect their outer world. Whether for pay or not, they join for Impact. These groups tend to be task-driven and externally oriented. We refer to them as External Change groups. (2) Purpose that supports individual group members, who in turn go out into the world and make a difference in their own unique ways. Examples include workshops, support groups, book clubs, hobby clubs, social organizations, and families. These groups are typically more socially and internally oriented and we call them Individual Support groups.

Purpose works in a tight creative dynamic with Bond. While Bond knits the group together from the inside, Purpose pulls the group forward and often outward in a common direction. Members caught up in Purpose might make statements like these:

- We move in the same direction.
- We influence each other.
- We count on each other.

Purpose statements are deeply informed by what the group intends to do in the World, as reflected in the World loop of the model discussed in the next chapter. The world out there gives the Group its reason to Bond and its Purpose. Nationally, we see Suzi's group as an example, or groups focused on reforming health care or education or safety. Locally, we see people claiming a seat at the table of civic dialogue. We see unions pursuing of the rights of their members. The possibility of making a difference in the world calls people together and forward in action.

We Move in the Same Direction

This statement is about both the direction and the movement; we know what we want and what we are doing together. We can see ourselves move and that builds our collective motivation; it reinforces our belief in our ultimate success. We are excited by discussions of Purpose and progress toward fulfilling it. We need to repeat, sometimes almost ritually, those discussions to reinforce our shared commitment. When we are not moving together or not moving at all, our sense of shared Purpose is at risk.

We Influence Each Other

We are defined not so much by our individual purposes as our collective Purpose, and to reach that we listen to each other. In the process, we refine what we are about together; we influence each other as we search for what we agree upon together. Without this, our shared Purpose is not clear, is not held deeply and collectively. When we have few opportunities to influence each other, we risk uninformed individual actions that damage the group. We need a process that assures us that we have our individual say in pursuit of group Purpose, and we need to know that our voice can make a difference. That is, because of what one person says, a group could alter its direction; one person can make a difference.

We Count on Each Other

In more extraordinary groups, it is a source of pride that we do not have to look to see if our teammates are beside us; we know they are. And we know this is a unique experience and one that we treasure. Counting on each other comes with shared participation in great outcomes in which each person carries out his or her role as the group expected. Often these are roles well discussed and rehearsed, but other times a member improvises and does so in a way that demonstrates her deep understanding of and dedication to the group and its Purpose. In doing so, she reinforces, "You can count on me." And counting on each other includes regular reminders that members of the group *are* counting on each other; that they must do this together; that they cannot achieve their Purpose separately.

The Creative Dynamic Between Bond and Purpose

Joining with others can be fulfilling beyond the limits of an isolated, individual experience. Grouping creates the possibility of building something larger than we ourselves imagined. With more minds, more muscle, more ideas, more motivation, more support, who knows what we might be able to do? Maybe discover a new place for ourselves in the world. Maybe create and sustain an effort for years making a huge difference in our organization. Maybe spark a magical group experience of the kind we would like to replicate again and again. These "maybes" are among the reasons people choose to Bond together united in Purpose in the creative dynamic shown in this next table.

The Creative Dynamic of Bond and Purpose

Bond: Our Shared Sense of Identity and Belonging	The Creative Dynamic ↔	Purpose: The Reason We Come Together
We know who we are together	↔	We influence each other
We create a safe space for each other	↔	We move in the same direction
We each play our parts together	↔	We count on each other

So far, this chapter has been an elaboration on the statements listed under Bond and Purpose above. The extraordinary groups we studied were notable in their interplay of these two needs, using Bond to support Purpose and vice versa. They saw and built upon the creative dynamic between these two needs. In Suzi's evolving campaign experience, the skills and talents of group members were employed in various ways to help their candidate successfully pass through the next hurdle, on the way to the national nomination. "At the very minimum," she recalls, "we behaved like coworkers and most of the time we were very dependent on each other. Different people had different skills, knowledge, leadership, and time. We'd leverage different items from different people as we needed to." The Woodlands Group offers another fine example of this.

A Shift in Purpose

We interviewed Frank, a thirty-year member of the Woodlands Group. He joined a few years after the group was founded in the late 1970s when ten men began meeting weekends once a quarter to discuss their roles as corporate training directors. Over the first fifteen years of its life, the group reshaped itself radically in membership, its structure changed, its Purpose evolved. Today the Woodlands Group is fourteen independent consultants, seven men and seven women plus spouses or partners. They still meet quarterly around North America for three days at a time, but their Purpose has shifted to exploring individual, organizational, and societal change. The Woodlands Group has intentionally altered its course, reflecting regularly on its Bond and Purpose. According to Frank, "The group has deepened in community, trust, and love. We've challenged ourselves about how well our ideas really work. We've become much more intentional about our purposes. We have suffered together, born each other's burdens. We are a small loving community that has made real contributions to each other and to other organizations."

In early years the Woodlands Group excluded visitors, including spouses, and met only for the benefit of individual members; during this period, it was an example of Individual Support groups. Thirty plus years later, the group now it invites significant others and visitors; it gives its time consulting to community organizations and government. This group's Purpose is now a combination of External Change and Individual Support. In this way, Woodlands is similar to other extraordinary groups we learned about, in which Purpose can shift, broaden, and deepen over time. As members listen to each other, they loosen their hold on their initial assumptions. A finer expression of Purpose can emerge, usually related to the former Purpose, but more compelling, challenging, and meaningful. Their strong intentions allow members to refine their Purpose as they move forward.

Frank believes these shifts in Bond and Purpose have been essential to the Woodland's Group's continuing vitality. His words—and words from other interviews—encourage us to emphasize the richness of the creative dynamic between Bond and Purpose, the two sides of the Group loop. We heard words like loyalty, love, history, suffering, commitment, performance, protection, ritual, frustration, habit, celebration, and competition. This fertile field between the group's internal relationship needs and the external task needs is full of possibilities. Possibilities fed by deeper needs behind the issues of the moment, possibilities that reach beyond the rational and the balance sheet toward larger needs members experience individually and collectively. And the tighter members are bonded in joint Purpose, the more powerful they will be out in the world.

Our field work also suggests that extraordinary groups are drawn to discovery, moving from known toward unknown. This mystery adds to the thrill of getting involved. Where individually members may not have the power to move, as a group they build power by reinforcing each other and moving beyond what they have ever done before. Our small group of two, as authors of this book, fits with this description. We have been excited by our exploration, not by knowing but by discovering our way. We have given each other courage to explore beyond our edges. This same pattern surfaced in Suzi's group, the Woodland's Group, and many other extraordinary groups we studied. The feelings within these groups are of latitude leading to creativity and discovery. Yes, there are boundaries provided by Purpose, but they are off in the distance, allowing plenty of room to move and discover.

Extraordinary groups embrace both the Bond and the Purpose sides of the Group loop. Seeing through this third view, it's about all six messages summarized in the table above, coming into play. Those intentions and actions come from seeing the whole Group loop and doing what's necessary to bring it to fuller life, perhaps creating a bit of transformation along the way.

In many ways groups of two to twenty are the world writ small, having close boundaries and dynamics that make them more manageable than the whole of the world. Within group boundaries, members can decide how they want to operate together. In groups, individuals do not have to take on the whole world by themselves. Members benefit from the belief that together they can make a difference—one that they could not make by themselves alone.

Guidance: Ways to Meet the Needs of Bond and Purpose

In Chapter Four, you thought about Acceptance and Potential separate from other Group Needs. But what happens when those very personal needs meet needs clearly centered in the group—Bond and Purpose? That's what the rest of this chapter is about; it joins you with the group, moving you from the detached "Me" to the connected "We." As in Chapter Four, we offer guidance on thinking about these two Group Needs that includes reflection questions and sample actions you can take to further your understanding.

Here's a typical situation that this chapter is written to address: Imagine that at work you have been asked to join a task force of ten people from different departments and positions in your organization. You approach the first meeting with many questions: What will they be like to work with? How should I present myself? What will they think of me? What do I want to accomplish? What will I gain from this? What should I wear? What will it cost me? A few minutes before your arrival, you are still considering these questions, many related to your self-Acceptance and Potential. Other members will arrive with their own Group Needs and similar questions in mind. Each of you will wonder how you will do and how this group of separate individuals might get something done together. If this sounds familiar, the rest of this chapter should be helpful to you. We begin with four suggestions useful in the integration of individual and Group Needs:

- Pursue service and learning.
- Facilitate group progress.

- Bring lightness and humor.
- Use conflict as a source of creativity.

As in the previous chapter, we will elaborate on each of these suggestions as well as offer questions for you to think about and actions for you to consider taking with your group. Look in Appendix A for exercises that give you further practice in meeting Bond and Purpose needs.

Pursue Service and Learning

What a graceful entry this first strategy provides! You are there to serve the group's Purpose; you are there to learn from others and the situation. Enter in this open manner as a model of generosity and service above self. Your positive intentions and constructive behavior are appreciated by your colleagues. You model openness to information and ideas along with commitment to the reason that brings you all together. Your example encourages others to do the same. Ideally, you enter a group with a good sense of yourself, who you are and what you need; you integrate those needs by looking at how you can be useful to the group and its purpose. Yes, you want to meet your own needs and you also want to meet the group's needs; you enter with that positive bias.

The selflessness of this strategy may challenge you, but we look to our sixty extraordinary groups for reinforcement. Time after time, when groups were highly successful, members were impressed by the generosity, the lack of ego, the openness of members. This infectious strategy opens the group to alternatives never considered in groups of more self-serving and all-knowing individuals.

Reflection Questions for You. Imagine intentionally building your excitement about joining a new group. Imagine entering in a positive spirit, leaning into the experience, with these questions in mind:

- What do you need to know or understand to be an effective member of this group?
- Who can help you learn what you need to know right now?
- How might you best serve what the group is doing?
- How might you contribute to the learning of other group members?

Continue to use these questions long after your entry to the group. Continue to serve; continue to learn.

Sample Actions with Your Group. Consider how you might practice acting differently for the sake of learning.

- If you are one to speak and act quickly and early, try an alternative approach. Instead of making statements to others, ask questions of others. What do you learn because of this shift in the way you normally do things?
- If you are one who typically sits back and observes, use your quiet time differently than you usually do. For example, note how other members demonstrate service to the group and learning from the group. What action might you take to be of service or actively encourage learning in the group?
- Ask the group to take some time to discuss what motivates members, why they choose to belong. Then ask what the group could do to meet more of these needs.
- As you listen to the group, consider what Group Needs members are trying to meet, what might be motivating

them to behave as they do. When you act, do so with other's needs in mind.

Facilitate Group Progress

You are in a group to help it move toward success. You may not be the leader or facilitator in a formal sense, but as a member you can help the group join in common action and Purpose. Like the previous strategy, this requires a group-serving rather than self-serving mind-set. The actions you take, the questions you hold are quite different from a more self-centered orientation. You see the group through the eyes of someone who wants the group to be highly successful; you want to see movement toward Purpose and unity within the group. You've read here what's required to create an extraordinary group and you can see the needs the group is trying to meet. Do your part to make this happen.

Reflection Questions for You. During a group meeting, keep these questions in mind; look for opportunities to use one or two you have never used before. Mentally replay a recent group meeting and review it from the framework of these questions:

- What did you do to help your group, a group meeting, or other group members be more effective? Be specific.
- What else could you have done to increase effectiveness?
- How does your behavior in this meeting fit with your typical behavior in meetings?
- What could you do next time to help this group progress?
- What would be rewarding to you about changing your behavior?

Sample Actions with Your Group. Of the many behaviors that might help a group progress, these pay particular attention to the group needs for Bond and Purpose:

- Before meetings, do your homework and arrive focused. Set aside concerns and distractions; keep group Bond and Purpose in mind.

- Show your support for other's participation by looking at them, using their names, asking for their points of view, building on what they say, praising their contributions, thanking them.

- Point out important common ground when you see it, helping the group understand what they have created together so far.

- Keep to the task or agenda that the group has agreed upon. Be exemplary in this regard. Don't hesitate to ask, or remind the group, of where they are in their work.

- Here is a set of useful questions for tracking group progress: Please help me understand—what are we doing right now? Who is going to do this? Who wants to help? What is it that we seem to be saying? Remind me again; how does this serve our purpose? What do you think we have learned from this? What have we accomplished so far? Make a point of using at least one of these questions in your next group meeting.

Bring Lightness and Humor

A difficult notion to capture, but important to note: A light touch wins out over heavy-handedness in exceptional groups. Just-enough, just-in-time. Just enough clarity. Just enough structure. Just enough role definition. Just enough boundaries.

Too much structure, role clarity, or definition of Purpose limits the creativity on which amazing groups thrive. "Just enough" creates a sense of unified Purpose and clarity, so that people feel grounded, safe, and free to move forward. Structure is most useful when provided just-in-time, just when the group needs it to move the work ahead. For example, rather than creating a long list of ground rules as the group gets started, consider creating one or two at a time, when the work calls for it.

Another aspect of lightness so apparent in extraordinary groups is delightful, joyful humor that happens spontaneously and generously. Its spirit is warm and appreciative of others, not cutting or competitive. Humor is creative, and creativity often springs from humor and its irreverence. With humorous observations comes the chance for a different take, a new idea, or an original thought. And humor often reflects a larger or balancing perspective on the situation. In effect, it says, "This isn't all as serious and important as we have been treating it . . . there is life outside this meeting and this work." Humor allows people to laugh at themselves and with each other, implicitly recognizing that as wonderful as we are, we are also flawed and funny. In that there is the suggestion of lightness and forgiveness. All of this supports groups surpassing their own expectations. A last point: When everyone is laughing together, at that moment they are all in the same place— just what groups need to increase their Bond and move forward toward Purpose together.

Reflection Questions for You. With one particular and important group in mind, consider these questions as a way to prepare for discussions in your group about how to go about the work.

- What do we currently use to structure our work? How are those elements working for us? Are there any that seem to get in our way?

- Who among our group seems to have the right skills or talents for the various things needing to be done?

- What do we really seem to enjoy about working with each other?

- How does humor show up in our group? On a scale of appreciate to competitive, where does it stand?

- What type of humor do you contribute? What intention do you have when you say things that cause others to laugh?

Sample Actions with Your Group.

- Encourage a discussion of the way your group works—the roles, the procedure, the measurements, the meetings. Check on member satisfaction with these various elements.

- Notice tendencies of members to control the group, and notice the impact when that happens. Talk with the group about when controls are more and less helpful. Discuss the effect of task controls on group membership.

- Notice how often your group joins in appreciating humor. Notice how light or heavy the atmosphere is in your group. What does this suggest the group needs more or less of?

- Make a point of interjecting humor into your group's work. Describe an experience with the intent of getting a laugh. Or make fun of yourself in a way you believe others will identify with. Or gently tease members who obviously enjoy that kind of attention.

Use Conflict as a Source of Creativity

We know conflict often results in miscommunication, hurt feelings, ego bruising, competition, and time wasted. All true, but conflict also presents the opportunity to consider separate ideas and how they might be joined. Disagreements and conflict are inevitable in groups and they are essential for innovation and collaboration. Our extraordinary groups showed a pattern uncharacteristic of other groups: they know that tension can lead to creativity; they lean toward it, pushing through the discomfort of the tension to the other side. They know that for the group to do its best work it first has to hear what members have to say and that members will disagree with one another. Relevant ideas left unsaid cannot be used by the group. The group's creative success depends on getting all ideas on the table. The risk is conflict that damages; the reward is creativity and deepened relationships. Conflict can lead to creativity; both are rooted in the interplay of disparate ideas. In conflict, two ideas compete for dominance. When conflict leads to creativity, two ideas join and break through to a new position.

Belief in the value of diverse contributions enables groups to pursue more constructive alternatives. Groups advance when members have confidence that conflict can be productive and creative, rather than destructive and polarizing. Early conflict of ideas is often at the source of transformation. The strength of individual members helps them to accept their current selves as they become their better selves. With that solid sense of self, they are more able to meet with others equally confident; they can display their ideas, be open to possibilities, and not be afraid of conflict.

Reflection Questions for You. Notice your comfort or discomfort with the idea that conflict can lead to creativity.

Think for a moment about recent conflicts before answering these questions:

- Why is disagreement useful to groups? Do you really believe that?
- What in your behavior shows that you respect other people and their viewpoints?
- What is the source of your personal comfort-to-discomfort with conflict?
- Who are the individuals you are more uncomfortable disagreeing with? Why?
- What are some responses you could use that show your respect for others while still disagreeing with them? How often do you use such responses?
- How could you demonstrate that you appreciate ideas that conflict with your own?

Sample Actions with Your Group. Individual and group discomfort with conflict is often deeply seated. Here are some small steps you can take to bring disagreements into the open so that they have the chance to spark creativity, accomplishment, and better relationships.

- Ask your group to read this chapter and Chapter Eight about embracing differences. Set aside time in the next meeting to discuss how the ideas apply to the group.
- Present the idea that conflict can lead to creativity. Ask the group how this notion might influence your work together.
- When someone in your group says something you disagree with, paraphrase that person to make sure you have really understood the point. Deliberately find out what the other person is interested in or needs.

- When you have demonstrated that you understand, state your view. If you can, highlight your common interests as well as where and why you differ. Then move on to a discussion of possible solutions that would be mutually agreeable. Use your joint commitment to your group's Purpose as the motivation to compromise when necessary.

- Ask your group to describe the kind of interactions it would like to have. What would produce feelings of being energized, connected, hopeful, and positively changed by the group's work together? Ask, What do conflict and disagreement have to do with what we've just talked about?

This Group loop of our model is particularly important. The extraordinary groups from our field study spoke often of a deep individual and collective sense of Purpose. So deep that members could count on each other to make good decisions on behalf of the group; they didn't have to always turn to a formal leader; they knew what to do next. And the Purpose bound them together tightly. As they celebrated Purpose and accomplishment, they grew even tighter. There is nothing like being in the trenches together to build connection, trust, and even love.

All of this works best when members enter the group well prepared for what they will face. Imagine a member joining a group with a healthy Acceptance of self and a sense of his individual Potential. In that group, he joins his talent and energy with that of other members; together, they get a sense of their shared Purpose and in the process begin to Bond as one entity, one group. In the coming chapter, all that concerted talent will be brought to bear on the world with the intention of making a difference.

6

CREATING CHANGE TOGETHER

"They called us the Blue Shirts," said Katie about a team of twenty-eight that implemented an automated patient medical record system in twenty-five family practice or specialty clinics. For three years, they wore blue shirts that identified them as the IT consultants. Two years later, says Sheila, "We are known by this name, even still." We had the opportunity to interview Sheila, who was the group's manager, and two members of the team—Katie and Catherine.

You'll catch the drift of their experience by considering the words and phrases used to describe their experience: "pushing people to their limits . . . tension . . . periodic, appropriate mutiny . . . high expectations . . . evolving . . . rewarding . . . fun . . . family-like camaraderie . . . tons of learning . . . recognition . . . a calling . . . people thought we couldn't do it . . . a sense of service." This intense and wonderful experience was transformative for all three women. For Catherine, "I've been launched into a world of diversity and now know how to navigate and adapt to different scenarios." Katie acknowledged that she did not have to be great at everything she did. "I realized where I was strong, but also learned how to ask for help and be vulnerable to others." Sheila has moved on to new leadership responsibilities. "I think I'm a more effective leader now. For example, I now know that not everyone is always going to be happy. I used to try to 'make it better' when there was tension. I don't do that as much anymore."

The Blue Shirts were a part of a larger effort that had significant Impact on patients and health care providers—allowing them immediate access to information and each other on a 24/7 basis. This could not have happened without their work in the clinics. Of their Purpose, Sheila said: "We were very clear about what we were trying to do. It was a very concrete thing to us. In the beginning, perhaps we were not as clear about the value we were really bringing. Over time, we felt better and more confident about what we were trying to accomplish. Every day, individuals made a difference—but it was always expressed in terms of the team." They also discovered that in clinic after clinic, as they focused on teaching and using the medical record technology, they had opportunities to see ways to improve the overall flow of work related to patient care. "We kept saying this project was a magnifying glass that enabled us to improve the process so the patient would have a better experience."

Reality for the Blue Shirts was filled with challenges. Four issues stand out:

- The scale of the work—they made their way through twenty-five clinics, spending four months in each location, guiding each clinic through the move from paper to electronic records so everyone could operate the new system.

- Resistance to change—as they tried to move the organization toward a more electronic approach, other health care organizations were un-installing similar systems because of staff resisting the new methods.

- A training curriculum that didn't fit—team members were frustrated by being required to teach a curriculum that was designed without full understanding of the circumstances faced by clinic staff.

- Turn-over within the Blue Shirt team—they had to learn how to motivate and retain bright, creative, sought-after people with well-developed technical and people skills when the work was repetitive and "other companies were recruiting away our teammates and paying twice as much!"

The team addressed these real world issues in several ways. Whatever the problem they ran into, "we'd analyze what happened and make changes." Sheila commented, "If we heard 'we're bored,' we'd change and give people more responsibility." To keep the job more satisfying, "we let people pick the sites where they worked to reduce commutes." Even still, they had to rehire half the team. Catherine recalls their push-back on the training curriculum and how "a combination of former teachers and nurses"—all Blue Shirts—"took over the curriculum and redid the design to make it work." Katie remembers that a group norm was clearly established: it was fine to voice concerns, "but only if you had an idea and were willing to contribute to fixing the problem." Doctors and nurses from other parts of the organization were brought in to see patients while clinic staff were involved in the training sessions; this was a big boost to the effort's credibility. Organized in subgroups that varied from clinic to clinic, team members were essentially self-organizing and handled most of their decisions without needing to check with management. But if a decision affected the whole group, it was opened up for whole-group input.

For three years, this group of highly diverse, skilled, and energetic members faced one Reality after the next. They did so because they believed in their mission and the benefits it would bring to patients and health care providers. As each clinic came online, they got to see their Impact. One clinic at a time, they recognized challenges, solved problems, saw tangible progress, celebrated success—then started all over again. And with each new beginning, they were better grounded, informed, skilled, and connected to one another.

Overview of Reality and Impact

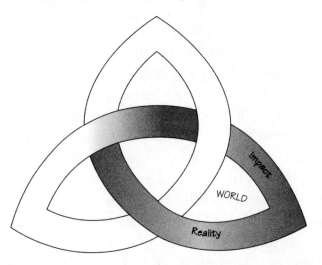

This chapter focuses on the last pair of linked Group Needs. It's about the group in action, attempting the change it wishes to make. External Change groups' ambitions intentionally include changing their external world. Individual Support groups are less focused on changing that world together, yet support their members as they go about living successful lives—often impacting the world. However these groups intend to have an Impact on the world, their actual accomplishment depends on how each group brings itself together in shared Purpose, and that depends on the individuals in the group, their awareness of what they bring and what they might become. In the Group Needs model, the Self loop empowers the Group loop, which in turn empowers the World loop. It is that last loop we will explore now.

By world we mean that bit of the entire world on which your group intends to have an Impact—the world closest to and most important to your group and its Purpose. This could be your extended family, your company, your local government, your state, or the planet. It may be multitiered, multistate, multifunctioned; it may be the competition, the union, the management, the Congress, the school, or the neighbors. Whatever your world is, your group's Bond and Purpose have led you to collectively invest in it.

The core dynamic within this World loop is the interplay between your group's ability to know and embrace its current world Reality—understanding and accepting the world as it is and how it affects you. This grounding is balanced by Impact, your intention to make a difference and your readiness to act. Logically, full appreciation of the world precedes taking action in it, but that is not always the case. As the Blue Shirt story illustrates, part of Reality is dealing with it as it comes, even when everything seems to be happening at once. You may be pushed toward Impact when you are not yet sure of what your Reality is.

Reality: Understanding and Accepting the World as It Is and How It Affects Us

Three group statements capture the importance of understanding and accepting your world as it is:

- We are alert to the world around us.
- We are intrigued with that world.
- We accept our reality.

Imagine yourself on the Blue Shirt team as you review these ideas.

We Are Alert to the World Around Us

The need for alertness flows from our most primitive roots. Being keenly aware day and night has allowed our species to survive. That survival need and its necessary alertness continue into the twenty-first century. Our reactions are significantly affected by perceived threats and opportunities. When what we sense is exciting and promising, we move more freely and expansively. When anxiety and danger are provoked, we move cautiously and protectively. Our choices between more expansive or protective stances come with consequences. A more open stance allows groups to turn their energy outward toward opportunity, acting to develop their interests, seeing their world through a more ambitious eye. When groups behave protectively, separating themselves from perceived danger, they typically turn their energy inward, erect barriers outward, and see their world through a shield. Regardless of the stance, when a group chooses to see the world, it must keep group Purpose and Bond in mind. Purpose and Bond contain the reasons the group formed in the first place and they are vital to holding it together.

We Are Intrigued with That World

Interviews with extraordinary groups reveal their curiosity about and fascination with their world. Even when they are greatly disturbed by it, they cannot easily put it aside. Like it or not, their world engages them and that engagement feeds group action: Action to learn more about their world so they will not be caught unprepared; action that takes advantage of their special insights. Where an ordinary group might see risk and peril, an extraordinary group can see opportunity.

The intrigue with the world is about fascination, curiosity, and engagement; it is not about judgment. Judging your world early on limits access to it and your options within it. When a group "knows" what is going on, it has less reason to explore what else might be going on. When a group "knows" its competitors are wrong, the group has good reason to dismiss the competition and all their ideas. When the group "knows" its product strategy is right, there are fewer reasons to explore what's happening in the marketplace today. Without the curiosity of intrigue, we have fewer reasons to learn, and that affects the actions we take to understand our Reality more deeply.

We Accept Our Reality

A group alert to its world and intrigued with it is in an excellent position to accept it. Not accept as in, "We give up and want our world to be that way," but accept as in, "We understand and appreciate that this is the way our world works right now." World change is best preceded by group agreement on what, in the world, is currently going on. When a group disagrees on what is happening in its world, actions are likely to be disjointed and disabling for the group. Why? Members don't share a common sense of Reality. The group lives in this complex world; it is not an elaborate case study that is analyzed from a distance. The group must take pragmatic steps to learn more about its world. High Impact begins with shared acceptance of the current Reality. By looking straight on into the heart of it, your group will be far more effective when it crafts its strategy about how to move ahead.

Impact: Our Intention to Make a Difference and Our Readiness to Act

A group intending to make a difference through concerted and collective action is likely to agree to the importance of these three statements:

- We want to improve our world.
- We need each other to make a difference.
- We are powerful together.

You are in a powerful position to act when your group's desire to have an Impact on its world is backed up with understanding of the current Reality and grounding in your Bond and Purpose, with members who are self-accepting and aspire to their Potential. Meeting this combination of needs puts the group squarely behind the changes it desires to make in the world. As you read on, look for reflections of the Blue Shirts' group experience.

We Want to Improve Our World

You know what your group's Reality is. Now, what is the Reality you want to create? Discomfort with the status quo is not motivation enough to constructively change it. Solid group action needs to be preceded by some imagining of, then plans for, what the group wants to make different. What would your group like to be celebrating in seven months or seven years or seven generations? For a moment, look over the fence separating the practical from the impractical; dream of what might be. In your heart, how do you want to see this world changed and improved? Not in your head, but in your heart of hearts, where motivation to act resides. When your group imagines and reaches together, it unites in spirit. Dreaming together gives expression to the long-ings held by individuals and now shared with the group, aiding your collective clarity on what you want to do together. When the group creates a vision of the world it wants, it readies itself for action in the present.

We Need Each Other to Make a Difference

Extraordinary groups commonly delight in, not just what they are able to do but also, how members' unique accomplish-ments are interdependent and meld together to contribute to the success of the entire group. Achieving together is a spe-cial experience rooted in the integration of individual con-tributions. It's as if the work is genetically imprinted by those participating: Looking back, members might say, "It's our baby; we made this! We all contributed." The outcome would have been different with different members. Members realize their individual importance to their shared accomplishment. This comes out in celebration when you hear, "Look at what we did! We couldn't have done this without each other!"

We Are Powerful Together

Meeting each of the six Group Needs builds power and it comes to fruition in Impact. Power is about combining tal-ents and aspirations to make a difference in the world. As the group sees its Impact, so do each of the members; they each know what they contributed. They feel more powerful. When members *feel* powerful, they *are* more powerful, and this affects their behavior, generally making it more expansive and creative. The vitality present in the group, the way it has used its resources, the learning of members, the effectiveness of action—all of this lifts the power of a group and its Impact.

The Creative Dynamic Between
Reality and Impact

Combining our understanding of our current world with the pursuit of a better world requires empathy, even compassion. We read the outside columns of the table below separately, but we live them together, two sides of the World loop. On the left, we pursue deep understanding of the current realities of our world. On the right, we move toward the world we wish to create together. And, as the center column suggests, we do both: we simultaneously accept the world while changing it. At least that's what our extraordinary groups' actions suggest. Hold a vision of what you want while knee-deep in Reality. This is the creative dynamic; this third view deepens your clarity about the world while expanding your options. This larger view from the third position makes transformation possible.

Katie, Catherine, Sheila, and all their Blue Shirt colleagues constantly worked within this creative dynamic within each clinic and within the larger team as one organizational unit. In the clinics as they implemented a similar process and worked toward the same outcomes, each of the twenty-six settings required the team to flex, adapt, and

The Creative Dynamic of Reality and Impact

Reality: Understanding and Accepting the World as It Is and How It Affects Us	The Creative Dynamic ↔	Impact: Our Intention to Make a Difference and Our Readiness to Act
We are alert to the world around us	↔	We want to improve our world
We are intrigued with that world	↔	We need each other to make a difference
We accept our reality	↔	We are powerful together

apply their various talents given the way Reality showed up in each location. The same was true for the team as a whole as it responded to member turnover and fatigue. Reality had to be addressed, and it took the full team to not only deal with that Reality, but to push past it to achieve the desired organization-changing Impact.

Guidance: Ways to Meet the Needs of Reality and Impact

In the preceding two chapters, the Self met itself, then the Self joined the Group, and now the Group goes out into the World—joining all six Group Needs in the model. As the group of now bonded individuals frames its Purpose within the context of the real world, all three loops of the model intersect. To help this happen, our four suggestions are

- Risk making your world a better place.
- Set clear goals with flexible plans.
- Face into adversity and resistance.
- Keep the group together.

The remainder of this chapter builds these suggestions with reflective questions for you to consider and sample actions you might take. And don't forget to look in Appendix A for exercises that take you step-by-step toward a better understanding of your world.

Risk Making Your World a Better Place

Note your first reaction to this first suggestion. Many of us have learned to step away from this grand dream—even though it is exactly what we would like to do! This strategy asks you to step back into that world-changing intention, that inspired feeling, you may have carried years ago. Return to hope and back it with action. This stance toward the world informs your actions. There is no doubt that you already have intentions toward the world and they profoundly affect what you see, do, and feel. We know, and our extraordinary groups know, that right action backed by positive intent works wonders. The same action backed by cynicism, fatalism, or pessimism produces quite a different result. So our first suggestion is a commitment of the heart: "I intend to make this world a better place." Try it on. If it fits, you are living one of the critical ingredients of progress.

Most great groups build on their members' desire to positively influence, to make a difference, to have an Impact on others and their world. This desire is about contribution, power, recognition, and legacy. Helping a group step up to these aspirations can be a challenge that requires a willingness to risk disappointment or failure. Earlier, we urged you to intentionally reach beyond in-the-moment practicality to dream a bit, to see your work in a grand way—and that is what the group must do too. This often comes about by engaging the group in dreaming, envisioning, and expressing what that better place looks like. In the same way, your group will consider two questions: What change do we envision for our world? And how will we bring that change about? Heartfelt collective answers to these questions build confidence to face the risk involved.

Reflection Questions for You. Considering these questions will center you for related discussions in your group. Notice the bias of the questions toward possibility and progress. Consider these questions based on your wide experience with groups, thinking particularly of groups that were more successful.

- What have you seen other successful groups do that allowed them to change their worlds?
- When have you been a group member truly invested in bringing about change? Why were you so invested?
- What are your key motivators when it comes to making a difference in the world?
- What regularly blocks you from stepping up to make your world a better place?
- What would you like to see yourself doing regarding the above questions that you do not now do?

Sample Actions with Your Group. Again, use the same optimistic bias we saw in your reflection questions. But this time it's the group's turn to think positively.

- Discuss ways in which your group could intentionally make its world a better place. Build a list of the specifics you want to see; mark those items where you can have the greatest Impact. Decide what needs to be done next.
- Ask that the group consider what members need in the way of world change for this to be a satisfying endeavor in which to invest themselves. Keep notes on this and then select a need or two that appears widely felt. Then together figure out what members could do in concert to meet those needs.
- Initiate a discussion about how your group is currently impacting its world, imagining that some higher authority seriously asked the group to do so. How would fulfilling this be for individual members? What would make it more so?

- Given your group's Purpose, what Impact would be most inspiring or make group members most proud?

- Encourage the group to discuss what members could do within the group to make their effectiveness outside the group more likely.

Set Clear Goals with Flexible Plans

When people are clear about the world they want to create around them, the question quickly becomes: How? Most of us schooled in the ways of groups believe that plans and strategies are critical tools for marshalling group's collective talent, knowledge, and energy. Our interviews shed a different and contrary light on that notion. The only aspect of typical planning methods that consistently surfaced as important was setting clear, inspiring, attainable—yet challenging—goals. Focused strategies, detailed plans, established procedures, or working agreements were not consistently cited as important by these extraordinary groups.

Instead, people spoke of the need for clear goals that stretched people and flexibility in attaining them—especially in situations where circumstances kept changing. A common comment: "Strategies could change, but goals stayed the same." Clear and sustained goals allow members to know individually and together what they intend to do to change their world. Then members can adapt as needed to respond to or take advantage of shifting circumstances.

Reflection Questions for You. Goals and plans are at the heart of what most organizations talk about—along with objectives and procedures, roles and rules. Consider your own reactions to all of this.

- How important are goals in your life? In your work? Why is there a difference between these answers—if there is?

- When have goals served you particularly well? Describe two or three instances. As you think about your answers, do they fit with the ways you generally describe yourself?

- How planful is your group? Will you have the ability to adapt your strategies as circumstances change?

- How do you like being part of a planned group effort?

- How planful are you—apart from the group? How natural is planning for you? If you are not a planner, what do you do instead? How effective is that for you?

Sample Actions with Your Group. Most groups recognize the need for goals at some level—otherwise, why do members come together? However, harnessing collective action toward goals can be challenging.

- Push the group to set goals to achieve the Impact for what you want to accomplish together. Hear from all members.

- When setting goals, check for clarity and support across the group. Assure goals are clear, doable, and challenging. Make sure these goals will fulfill the group's Purpose and desired Impact.

- Consider the current Reality the group faces in carrying out these goals. Do a deep assessment of barriers and the support needed to overcome those obstacles.

- Ask the group to discuss how members can support each other on the way to goal accomplishment.

- Develop a "Plan B"—what to do to continue to reach your goals if your Reality shifts.

Face into Adversity and Resistance

Time and time again extraordinary groups cited "a challenge" as a big factor in making their experiences compelling. The challenge of doing something huge, important, new, or difficult galvanizes people, inspires and requires them to step up. In such situations, groups must understand the Reality they face as they step up. Turning away from the forces arrayed against the group does not serve. Our interviews touched on a wide range of resistance and adversity: physical hardship, cultural diversity, deliberate miscommunication, lack of technical skill, language barriers, poverty, limited life experience, egos, and lack of funding. We suspect you could double this list. Each adversity offers an intriguing challenge for your group as you face resistance and drill down into Reality.

Denying the resistance of others will also not serve your group. Resistance is natural and usually the indication that your efforts have engaged something important. Extraordinary groups expect and enjoy rising to such challenges; it's part of what Bonds them. In politically sensitive organizations, groups are faced with bringing along "those other people" who "don't see things our way." These others can be any-one: management, a department, a person, a small group of employees, a group of citizens, a new boss. In each case, those others are a part of the Reality the group must face. A group's challenge is often embracing and holding resistance, accept-ing its Reality by respecting and honoring where this resis-tance comes from. This does not mean caving in to it, but rather learning from it in order to move ahead.

Reflection Questions for You. Resistance always comes from people. It may be reified in rules, but there are people and decisions behind those rules. And resistance is primarily about feelings—usually fear of some sort of loss. Notice your own resistance, your own reactions to adversity.

- Think about adversity and how it shows up in your work, community or personal life. Are there patterns in the way you typically respond to these challenges?
- Which of the Group needs are most likely to come up for you when you resist? Acceptance or Potential? Bond or Purpose? Reality or Impact? What fears or worries trigger your resistance?
- When you see other people resisting, how does that affect you? Do you find your own resistance being activated by theirs?
- Can you think of examples from a group you are currently part of in which you showed resistance? What did you do and why? How effective was that for you? For others?

Sample Actions with Your Group. One of the keys to succeeding in the face of resistance is to understand and respect it. Help your group members talk openly about resistance they see in others and in themselves.

- Be a group of learners. With others from your group, meet with those who resist your efforts; listen to them; ask lots of questions and collect what you learn in response. Demonstrate that you understand their views. Remember that understanding does not mean agreement.
- Deal with resistance as normal. In a group meeting, anticipate the resistance you expect. Build a list. Decide what you want to do about the items on your list.
- On a regular basis, assess the Reality your group faces, recognizing that circumstances change. Talk about Reality in

group meetings. Together determine whether shifting circumstances translate into something as serious as adversity. If so, how will you collectively respond?

Keep the Group Together

Groups intent on changing their world are wise to pause periodically to check-in on what holds members together. In our view, the answers lie within the six Group Needs. People show up physically, emotionally, and spiritually when their needs are being met. They pull away when their needs are neglected. In extraordinary groups, members act in ways that keep the group together. When designated leaders try to handle this task alone, it doesn't work. Anyone in the group can help build relationships, encourage learning, praise accomplishment, listen to contrary ideas, offer assistance, ask questions. Designated leaders have a significant role, but in only half of our extraordinary groups were designated leaders cited as very important to the group's success. Instead it is what group members do together that coalesces them into an effective unit. Said differently, every member acts in leader-like ways; each feels responsibility for creating a cohesive group that moves toward success.

The potential for Impact on the world is a great motivator, but it is not enough because it only meets one of the six Group Needs that drive people in groups. Groups need to attend to the other five as well to increase the likelihood of great results and a transformative experience. Groups only focused on Purpose, Reality and Impact often lose heart—because so much of heart is in the other three needs: Acceptance, Potential, and Bond. Meeting all the task needs and none of the relationship needs sucks the life out of the group.

Reflection Questions for You. Returning to questions like these regularly makes it more likely your Group Needs will be met within the group. Give voice to your answers in the group. Keep the six Group Needs in mind as you answer these questions.

- What do you need from this group that you are regularly getting? What do you need and seldom get?
- How does having your own Group Needs met impact your day-to-day behavior in the group?
- What Group Needs do you see at play among other members in the group?
- What could you do in the group to better meet their Group Needs?
- What are the primary bonds that hold this group together?
- What are your responsibilities for keeping the group together? How do you fulfill this obligation?

Sample Actions with Your Group. The Group Needs model is a useful tool for focusing the entire group on what the members, individually and collectively, need.

- Review the Group Needs model with your group. Ask members to cite examples of where these needs have been recently met. Then ask where needs have regularly been frustrated. Use all of this information to decide what the group might do next to better meet these needs.
- Help your group spend time reviewing its accomplishments, large and small. Occasionally, turn this into a real celebration. Celebrate work progress at least as often as the group is critical of progress. Learn from your success and learn from your failures.

- Support the group by setting aside time for members to vent their frustrations with the group itself or the world on which the group is trying to have an Impact.

- Deal with group frustrations as normal. Do not expect perfect projects, perfect performance, or perfect meetings. Be accepting of the circumstances you face; build from there. Forgive mistakes and learn from setbacks and failure. Do not focus on punishment. Never blame.

- Support wide involvement of group members; encourage people to take on a variety of roles. Do not rely on the few to carry the many forward. Rely on the many; expect them all to initiate, to take responsibility, to lead. Talk about the importance of full-engagement and shared leadership.

Of course, recognizing Reality and having an Impact on the world are just two of the six Group Needs being met in group action. The more members attend to all Group Needs, the better the group will perform. As important as Reality and Impact are to the continued life of a group, our interviews found that extraordinary groups don't just "keep their eye on the ball." They instinctively keep their eyes on *all* the balls, in this case, all the Group Needs. We encourage you and your groups to consciously scan your selves, your members, your world—deciding what is important again and again. The more Group Needs are met, the more likely something transformative will occur. Chapter Seven illustrates this dynamic with several examples from our field study.

7

THE HEART OF TRANSFORMATION

By now, you should have a firm understanding of the three sets of paired Group Needs within the Self, Group, and World loops and the creative dynamics that exist within each loop. We hope that the stories we've shared and the guidance we've provided in the last three chapters have helped you see how you might put the Group Needs model to work. We now move to the next level of complexity: considering all three loops together. When cross-loop needs are met in one group experience, they intersect at the heart of our complete model. Transformation becomes more likely and can carry a more powerful impact.

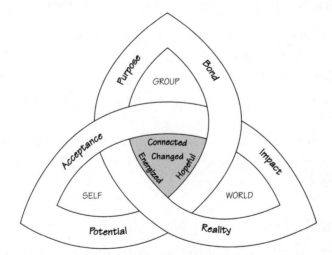

As you remember from Chapter Three, by *transformation* we mean a fundamental shift in individual perception that accelerates behavior change and personal vitality. This chapter builds on the thoughts presented there. It elaborates on what we see as the heart of transformation—the meeting of multiple Group Needs—across our model—at once. We offer six shorter stories that illustrate the way a group can be transformative. But first, here's a quick reminder about how transformation occurs in groups; it

- Happens one person at a time
- Seldom happens simultaneously for an entire group
- Is private and can't be guaranteed
- Can be encouraged
- Is more likely when more Group Needs are met
- Results in people feeling changed, energized, connected and hopeful

Six Stories at the Heart of Transformation

The rest of this chapter tells of six groups in which at least two or three Group Needs were met, crossing two or three loops. We offer three stories from the work place and three from people's personal lives, illustrating different combinations of all six Group Needs. For each story, we'll identify the Group Needs that seem most present to us. But don't let our choices narrow your interpretations. Read these six stories with these questions in mind:

- Which of the six Group Needs do you see at work?
- What is your sense of the transformation reported in each story? How dramatic or subtle does it seem? Is it likely to be visible to others or more privately held by the person experiencing it?

- Why do you imagine that people in the stories feel changed, energized, connected, and hopeful? If you put yourself in their places, do you imagine that you might have felt the same way?

- How does this story fit with your life experience? What memories does it trigger? What was transformative for you in that remembered group experience?

- What did you learn from the story that might be useful to you as you consider applying the Group Needs model in your work or personal life?

These questions will help you see the stories through the loops and needs of the model, making it more likely you will use this view on groups in your work and life. Mark this page and the previous one; we will ask you to refer back to these questions after each story.

When Acceptance Joins with Bond

The common pairing of needs of Acceptance and Bond extends from the individual to group and back again. A sense of belonging to and connection with a group inspires observations such as "This is my tribe, my 'real' family. These are my people." The individual is nurtured within the group, gains insight and risks within the safety the group provides. In this way, groups are powerful and enlivening teachers; their lessons can last a lifetime.

Lessons That Last a Lifetime

Take the case for Eric, an American now forty-three years old and living in Mumbai, India, and still influenced by a peak group experience in his early teens. Thirty years ago he joined a team of junior high boys at the local YMCA. This team played different sports, sold candy, participated in talent shows, and used the Y as a place to hang out. Looking back on this time, he says, "It became a very important group in terms of my identity, positive use of time, attitudes toward the world . . . and toward girls. We were a very diverse group of all different colors: Japanese, Korean, Polish, East Indian, Irish. I didn't know most of them when I joined." Humor was important to the boys. Not all that great at sports, Eric remembers learning about wit from this group: "We couldn't slam dunk a basketball, but we sure could slam dunk a joke."

When we asked him how he saw himself changed because of the group, he said, "It's a matter of skills and confidence in interacting with people. We could talk about almost anything. After three years together, I knew I could be appreciated and liked outside my family. Consistently." Later he added, "I don't know if we knew we were growing, but this felt good and I was where I belonged." Looking back thirty years, Eric knows he learned some lasting lessons. And, in spite of living half-way around the world, he is still actively in touch with some of the boys-now-men who were a part of his Y team. And who knows how much that early diverse group influenced his life and career in international journalism?

Which of the six needs do you see in play in Eric's life? Turn back to our earlier questions on pages 124 and 125 to gain more from Eric's story.

When Bond Joins Reality

Bond and Reality can come together to connect a group facing hard challenges in the external world, bonding the group even more tightly.

An Online Support Group

Marguerite, grappling with a challenging situation related to the health of her daughter, joined an online group and connected with other parents facing the same circumstances. For two and half years, her daily participation in this group has, as she says, "made my life livable! It boils down to that. If no one gets it—your spouse, your family, your friends—you are at a loss." Marguerite's Reality is that her beautiful, seven-year-old daughter has five mental health diagnoses, including being bipolar. Marguerite says, "When I went online, all these other parents across the country told the same story. I was crying and crying to know I was not alone. It was an incredible relief!"

Online five or six times a day, Marguerite uses the group for medical advice, information on medications, emotional support, suggestions for how to deal with the school system, and advocacy. She sees it as "one-stop shopping. Someone will know the answer to the question; someone will have been through it." Even though she has never met any of the group members in person, her Bond with them is palpable. "I quit for one year," she told us. "But I found I was too isolated and needed more support that no one outside the group could offer. So I got back online and got so much support!" Messages quickly came in saying, "Welcome back! How is your daughter?" Through the online community, Marguerite's daughter has even found an e-mail buddy in another state, a child her age with similar challenges. With huge social issues to face at school, the two communicate online and talk on the phone, an opportunity that helps both children feel appreciated and less alone.

Through her Bond with this group, Marguerite became more effective in handling her Reality. And, what other Group

Needs do you see at play? Review the six; you may be surprised. Imagine how they contributed to Marguerite's more transformative moments. Also consider the questions we posed early in the chapter.

When Acceptance Joins with Bond and Reality

Whether Art imitates Life, or it's the other way around, we think that the old television program *Cheers* had much to say about extraordinary groups. That cast of flawed and lovable characters would assemble in the tavern four to five nights a week. The group seldom talked about it, but we viewers could see that the Bond they shared allowed them to go out and deal with the realities of their own worlds. And occasionally, some flash of self-Acceptance would arrive for various characters. Transformative? In a quiet way, building a pattern of personal support from a group implicitly clear on what held it together. We think that Rob's story illustrates a similar combination of Group Needs—but in a vastly different setting.

An Alaska Raft Trip

In the summer of 2007, Rob joined a group of fifteen others for a three week raft trip in a remote part of Alaska. No one on the trip knew everyone; several were former Outward Bound guides; eight of the ten adults had attended college together. Five children of some group members, ages eleven to twenty, came along. This group paddled two hundred miles of river through multiple mountain ranges and indescribably beautiful wilderness. They arrived by land, flew out by plane and didn't see other humans for eleven days.

For Rob, aged fifty-seven, the trip was unforgettable: "We were a tribe—we moved across the land and down the river together." In the first week, one boat flipped, tossing four people into the rapids—including a mother, father, and daughter; a family that had tragically lost their other daughter some years before. Rob remembers, "This was very scary. Yet we were very successful in how we handled the crisis— we only lost one paddle! This brought us together more and helped us respect the challenges and dangers on the river." The remote setting was an undeniable Reality. "We absolutely depended on one another to survive. If we didn't work well together, we wouldn't make it. This was not contrived." Knowing himself and what he could contribute, Rob brought his rafting skills and his wilderness savvy. He is a natural when it comes to building relationships. And he trained to make sure he was physically strong enough for the trip.

The trip reconfirmed Rob's belief in the transformative effect of time in the wilderness—something that had slipped in his busy life. He sees the cross-family and cross-generational relationships that were built on the trip and he expects them to last. Rob says, "I don't really know how to articulate this. I have no current religious life and only a small spiritual practice. But this experience involved God. Our spirits were touched. The earth revealed all of its beauty to us. The universe allowed us to have this extraordinary experience together. We were blessed."

What particularly strikes you about Group Needs met in Rob's story? And which answers to the list of questions at the beginning of this chapter are particularly intriguing? How can you imagine that the feelings of being changed, energized, connected, or hopeful materialized for the rafters?

When Potential Joins with Purpose

The next story links the Self and Group loops in the transforming combination of Potential and Purpose. This linkage further clarifies for an individual just what his Potential might be, and at the same time feeds the group Purpose. Let's learn more about this through Chris.

Youth Group Trips to Mexico

 Since age twenty, Chris has traveled to Mexico once a year on church missionary work. Now twenty-eight, for the last seven years as an employed youth pastor, he has led groups of junior high school students on one-week missions to Puerto Peñasco, Mexico. "On my first trip, I went thinking that I had something great to offer. Now I see it completely from the opposite point of view—I am deeply humbled by all I have learned from my friends in Peñasco." Chris's sense of who he is has been transformed by how he sees the Purpose of the trips, and vice versa. Yes, the Purpose has to do with faith-based service to those less fortunate, but at a larger and more significant level it is about "helping young people understand the global ramifications of uniting with other cultures, so that they understand their humanness in a world context." Reflecting on his own emerging Potential, Chris is very clear: "This has forever changed me. I will never think the same way again, never watch a news report in the same way. I am drastically changed by the warmth of the Mexican people. I am working on my Spanish. I am learning where their joy and faith come from. I am learning to be a global thinker. I want to know more about the world than what CNN tells me."

Chris's perception of the world changed and that changed him. What else do you note about this story related to his Group Needs, the four feelings, and transformation? Can you find similar experiences in your own life? Apply the questions at the beginning of this chapter to Chris's situation.

When Purpose Joins with Impact and Bond

The link between Purpose and Impact is common in workplace organizations as people form groups to change some aspect of their internal or external world. Magda's story began there but, to her delight, added the additional element of Bond among group members.

Culture Change in 190 Countries

In the international division of a food products company, Magda—who is Polish—led a virtual team of herself and three external consultants, each from a different country: Germany, Ireland, and the United States. Their initial Purpose was to design and implement a diversity and inclusion program that would increase business results in 180 countries outside the United States, affecting 90,000 people. After four years, Magda knows the Impact of their work was much more than she originally anticipated. Surpassing her expectations for results, their team helped this global company become a more open and welcoming place to work. A place where "employees were given the courage to demand that the organization change and where individual leaders can truly impact the culture" of their facilities. For the company's U.S. division, such Impact was far more familiar and less revolutionary. But within the 180 countries on which Magda's team focused, the Impact on their world was both unusual and profound.

In addition, Magda knows that "these people became my friends." Mostly connected through technology, due to their geographical distance, she comments that the four of them "always felt a 'part of the family'—this was not just a relationship between a client and three contractors. I have never experienced this before—and I work with a lot of consultants." This quartet of four members, who have done amazing work and built a solid friendship with one another, has been the source of great learning for Magda. "I was brought up to think that people are equal." Through the course of this work, Magda realized that she was looking at the situations of others through her own fortunate life experiences. "What I didn't understand was that people need to *have* equal opportunity." She has applied this insight to the diversity and inclusion work and to her personal life. "In many conversations with my family or my friends, I now react quite strongly when issues of discrimination come up. I try to explore this with them in a positive way. I am conscious of modeling this for my daughter. Some time ago, I wouldn't have done this."

Notice the energy generated by a tight fit between Purpose and Impact. How does the addition of Bond augment the power of the experience? Where do you see transformation? Review those now-familiar questions on pages 124 and 125 as a way to think more about Magda's story.

When Purpose and Impact Join with Potential

Here is a story about powerful and concrete results—for the citizens of one region and for one of the key players in a group. Nine years ago, when this story took place, it was as though a stone was tossed into quiet lake water. The ripples of Impact continue to this day.

Online Services for Citizens

 In the late 1990s, the building officials of four nearby cities had lunch and decided that it was time to get serious about two things: using technology to help meet citizen needs and partnering to do so. At the same time, a group of city managers put together a regional strategic plan for online services. John was tapped to coordinate the first project within this effort through a cross-boundary management team. The effort resulted in mybuildingpermit.com—an "e-government" system to allow citizens from four adjacent cities to secure their building permits online. Nationwide, this was considered cutting-edge work at the time. It was accomplished within only sixteen months from initiation to issuing the first online permit—a notable achievement given the complexity faced by the team. John shared with us that since its inception, mybuildingpermit.com has issues over 77,000 permits. The Impact of this effort? "Our very conservative estimate is that contractors have saved over $3 million in direct operating and labor costs." Imagine working collaboratively across four separate public sector organizations—each with its own city council, city manager, building division, permitting process, IT function, and computer equipment. By fulfilling their Purpose, John and his team set the stage for even wider community Impact, as they quickly moved on to developing other ways to connect citizens to local government through the use of computers.

Looking back it's easy to see a larger Purpose than simply creating an electronic permit process. The vision of the city managers and the building officials opened up a whole new way for citizens to engage with and be served by their local governments. This was a powerful notion whose time had come. In 2004, John stepped into the next phase of his Potential. He found himself executive director of a newly formed organization, sponsored by nine cities, and tasked with providing efficient and cost effective Web-based services to its constituents. John's agency has gone on to successfully launch a total of seven regional Web service portals ranging from parks and recreation to human services to online mapping to government procurement and online job applications. In 2009, this alliance was serving forty-three public agencies.

As its leader, John continues to build on the lessons learned through the first project, and is even more committed to collaboration, engagement of stakeholders, and "leading without authority from the back of the bus." As he thinks about previous roles in his career, where he had more defined authority, John now sees that "I enjoy living in the gray—where things are ambiguous. I love being involved with new things and leveraging teamwork to do things that have never been done before. In this work, it's all about timing, bringing in the right talent at the right time, and relationships, relationships, relationships!"

We think John's story is a great way to wrap up Part Two. It's filled with accomplishment at the levels of Self, Group, and World; we know it was transformative for John and has had a powerful Impact on the way four cities and other jurisdictions go about serving citizens. What would you add to that? Look back one more time to our opening questions; they can help you reveal even more meaning in John's story.

As you have read stories from our extraordinary groups, we suspect that you have thought of a few of your own that could have been part of this chapter. Your stories could be considered through the same questions about Group Needs and transformation that we regularly asked. In doing so, you would require yourself to look through the loops of the Group Needs model; you might understand what happened in your story differently as you focused on these Group Needs. That in turn might suggest an action that would have been useful or an action you might take in the future. When you act to meet these Group Needs, the dynamics within the group change, and its Impact on the world changes as well.

Each of the stories we present—in this and other chapters—took place in ordinary groups of people who were not intentional about meeting anyone's Group Needs. Imagine what might occur in your groups if members consciously thought about helping others meet their needs for Acceptance, Potential, Bond, Purpose, Reality, and Impact? What if every time a group meets, the meeting design reflected two or more of these needs? Consider the difference it might make in the quality of conversation, if members were mindful of the six Group Needs. We predict that as you and other members satisfy Group Needs that cross the lines of Self, Group, and World, the "magic" of transformation will appear. And that as a result, you and others will be able to declare that you are changed, energized, connected, and hopeful.

Part Three takes you deeper into this territory.

Part Three

SHARING LEADERSHIP

Since you have read this far, you've no doubt thought many times about what might be required of you if you were to put all that we've offered so far into action. Know that whatever you decide to so, some level of risk, perseverance, patience, and leadership will be necessary. And not always leadership in the traditional and solitary mode. What's called for is shared leadership, where you and others are willing to step forward to offer what is needed in the moment.

Chapter Eight helps you understand what it is like to be in a group that sees differences as essential to creative and productive outcomes. If we had to name the largest detractor from becoming an extraordinary group, the inability to embrace differences would be a contender for first place. Our experience is reinforced by what we learned in our field study about the extraordinary groups that understood that their differences were essential to their success.

Chapter Nine speaks directly to those with the role of designated group leader. Although we highlight this one role, group facilitators and members will also find the content useful. We emphasize ways that leaders can conduct themselves in order to embrace differences, create full engagement, and share the leadership of a group.

Chapter Ten pulls the book to a close with a set of final observations about the points that stand out to us from our three-year journey with *Extraordinary Groups*.

8

EMBRACING GROUP DIFFERENCES

Ah, differences! The spice that makes life and relationships interesting, surprising, and compelling. And the source of irritations that can cause disruption, turmoil, and pain. When it comes to groups, both of these statements are true. Experience in most groups teaches hesitancy about encouraging diverse opinions. Extraordinary groups offer a different lesson. There, members are more likely to lean into their differences. In this chapter, we encourage you to do exactly that—lean in to explore and learn from the wide array of viewpoints and experiences present in your group. We ask you to think more deeply about the tension differences create and the way this tension can become the source of creativity and connection. We report on how differences represent an essential ingredient of extraordinary groups and describe the way that the six Group Needs are met when team members actively embrace those differences. We then offer guidance for how you can first prepare yourself and then encourage your groups to learn from and capitalize on the rich diversity brought by members.

On the Value of Differences

When a group forms, each person's age, skill, gender, relationships, religion, ethnicity, personality, sexual orientation, professional background, style, upbringing, education,

physical capacity, and life experience arrive at every meeting. This broad range is on display as members consciously
and not so consciously attempt to meet their Group Needs.
In ordinary groups, there is a well-recognized pattern:
in pursuit of what joins people together, members often
skirt over what sets them apart. They avoid their separate
edges in an effort to create a harmonious experience. In
extraordinary groups, the opposite takes place. Members
are curious and want to know more about their differences.
Individuals are encouraged to contribute their unique
knowledge, skills, feelings, and opinions. They speak passionately to points they see as important. They step into this
hard work of careful listening and setting aside personal
bias or the desire to be right. They open themselves up to
the often messy, confusing, and scary exchanges that can
presage a creative group outcome. They know that their
ability to build on those differences creates a unique
advantage for their group. They understand that embracing differences is not about resolving conflicts or winning
a debate; it is about welcoming and holding differences
in a nurturing way, so that they can be seen, understood,
and used as a resource to achieve a group's Purpose and
Impact. Full engagement requires this approach. Without
embracing differences, collaboration and innovation are
impossible.

How Extraordinary Groups Use Differences

We are more frequently hearing phrases such as "cross-
functional groups" or statements such as "we need to make
sure we've got the full range of perspectives included." There
is increasing recognition about the value of intentionally
including differences when inviting people to join a group.

We are learning to not just face the Reality of difference, but also build on it. This trend makes it even more important that all those unique perspectives inform the group and spark creativity. Obviously, taking advantage of the diversity brought by members is much more difficult in groups where people back away from the challenge of being open to different points of view.

Extraordinary groups cultivate a positive mind-set about differences, choosing to see them as intriguing, informative, and essential—rather than irritating, divisive, or threatening. In two-thirds of our collected stories, people identified the differences within their groups and the ability to express and work with these differences as critical to their success. The gist of their stories is this: First, since no two people are alike, group members necessarily see the world differently. Second, these differences cannot benefit the group when they stay in the background or threaten members when they enter the foreground. Third, if you want an extraordinary group experience, you must legitimize these differences; you must hold the differences for the group's consideration. And you must do this in ways that allow people to move forward together rather than pull the group apart. This capacity is a core distinction—a pivot point—between ordinary and extraordinary groups.

Before we offer our suggestions for how to build this capacity in your groups, we want to highlight two important concepts:

- Commitment to Purpose allows sorting out differences.
- Working with differences meets Group Needs.

To help us explore these two points, we offer another story from our field study.

Redesigning the Sales Process

In 1995, Nancy's company started losing customers to foreign competition. She was invited to join a cross-functional team that would redesign how their products were sold globally. Fifteen handpicked individuals were pulled from their regular jobs for this effort. "Subject matter experts in different fields were locked behind closed doors for three months." These individuals, with huge differences in background and position, immersed themselves in reams of information related to the product, the market, the organization, its systems, and input from customers and executives.

In the end, they recommended "completely revamping the structure of all units associated with sales." As their recommendations were accepted, Nancy recalls, "This design team morphed into an implementation team. We each started out wearing our functional hats and together became the pinnacle of what a team can achieve." She continued, "It was transformational at many different levels . . . it was like the blinders had been taken off. I saw that the world was bigger than I had previously thought. This required a flip in my thinking." Listening to Nancy, we could hear the depth of change this larger view of the world represented for her—and to all members of the team as they both respected what each person brought and created something larger than any one of them could have done alone.

Commitment to Purpose Allows Sorting Out Differences

Nancy's story fits with a pattern in extraordinary group experiences: Commitment to team Purpose creates the context for members to set aside their personal biases and self-interest for the good of the whole. When team members would find themselves caught up in their disagreements, "someone would say that we needed to step back and remember what we were all about. The objective was a real rallying point. The market place and the customers had shifted. We now had formidable competition forcing the complacency and arrogance out of our system. We were suddenly aware that we didn't have a divine right to 80 percent of the market."

Nancy saw that "people were willing to put the identity and success of our team ahead of their own sense of importance and individuality. The old hierarchy from Sales started to reduce their egos. A real eye-opening moment was when some of them realized that they would get to a certain point in the selling process "and then throw the sale over the fence." In other words, they would assume their job was done and let others who came next in the sales process fend for themselves. "At that point, there was an awareness of what it was like to be in another person's shoes. They finally realized that 'I am not the only one; this is not all about me!' People gained a sense that we don't do this alone." Bingo! Another shift in perceptions due to common Purpose. But notice that group members did not gain this insight in a splurge of generosity and team Purpose. No, they got there by initially putting themselves forward and facing the differences among the team.

When asked about how the group faced those differences, Nancy remembers that it wasn't necessarily pretty. "It included shouting matches and people storming out of the room. When that happened, we'd take a break. Sometimes we'd retreat into our reading material. When we reconvened, we'd acknowledge what happened, admit that there were no hard feelings, and get back into it." What enabled people to do this? "The integrity of each person, the sense of obligation to do this task—to sink our teeth into something really important for the company. And the recognition that no one was happy with the way things were. Everyone involved was trying to do what was best for the organization." Again, the importance of commitment to Purpose.

Working Through Differences Meets Group Needs

In our extraordinary groups, members made their way through sometimes volatile and messy clashes by reminding themselves that something marvelous could happen if they could just see it through. At some level people knew that fantastic results could not be achieved by a follow-the-rules-and-avoid-conflict approach. When asked to name three factors that made her team experience so outstanding, Nancy cited its quick ability to surface disagreements; letting go of right-and-wrong and ego; and a willingness to explore. As we examined other stories where diverse views and conflict were cited as important contributors to great results, we saw how the willingness to face into differences was a powerful means of meeting *all* six of the Group Needs. Prior to this recognition, we knew that commitment to Purpose was hugely important. But we hadn't seen so clearly the full power of embracing differences. We continue with Nancy's story to demonstrate this discovery about the five other Group Needs—Acceptance, Potential, Bond, Reality, and Impact.

Acceptance: Knowing and Accepting Ourselves for Who We Are. Nancy says that in an experience like hers, "You learned about yourself, how you show up, what your behaviors do to others. I was in a room with all these talented people. Some days were very humbling and I wondered 'why am I here?'" Later in the interview, she acknowledged, "I have a tendency to be my own worst enemy. But this experience showed me that I truly did belong with this team. It gave me an amazing sense of self-worth."

Potential: Sensing and Growing into Our Fuller and Better Selves. "There was such a willingness to explore. It felt like we were sitting on the edge of a new frontier, doing the cutting-edge thinking." Nancy knew this team was expanding her Potential. Also a musician, she knows "what the creative process is like in an arena that is expected to be creative. I hadn't experienced the creative juice in an organization before being on this team." As the team talked through members' different views of the future, "There was an amazing exploration to all the thinking and research we did. It was grad school level." When asked the degree to which this experience enabled her to learn new things in order to realize some of her Potential, she rated it as "a 38-point font! I thrive on learning new things and am interested in so many different things. Our experience really fed that part of me." Notice how tightly Nancy's fulfillment of her Potential is bound to the team's exploration of its differences. We heard this often in our field study.

Bond: Our Shared Sense of Identity and Belonging. Nancy saw her diverse team bonding as a whole and how their ability to challenge each other was a part of that process. "It was amazing to see how the team moved. The respect, enjoying each others' company, bringing out the best in each other, challenging each other. There was a real depth of feeling, a sense of 'I want to know more about your world and about you.'" As to her own experience, she simply stated that "It gave me a sense of belonging."

Reality: Understanding and Accepting the World as It Is and How It Affects Us. Nancy remembers the hard work that was required for some members to get beyond their well-established view of how things worked. People gradually came to understand that "this work was going to make a big difference—and that it was really about changing the corporate culture. And this was going to be really hard work!" The team's work "challenged people to think in terms of the whole process—from the first point of customer contact to the delivery and servicing of the product. Misconceptions were brought to light. People were so used to living in silos. They got to see what the world looked like from another point of view." Nancy saw the transformative Impact of examining the Reality of different views and how it triggered another "flip in thinking. That's what I was really watching. Some people were very uncomfortable and had a hard time. Some left because they couldn't handle the change in thinking. Those that stayed were willing to shift." Without the exploration of different views, they would not have been able to see the whole picture, the whole Reality.

Impact: Our Intention to Make a Difference and Our Readiness to Act. The cross-functional membership of Nancy's group assured that different perspectives of the whole process would be at the table so that their recommendations would be credible and actionable. Out of those built-in differences and the way in which the team faced them came important results. For the first time in the company's history, a documented process that would allow that process to be intentionally managed. A decision to co-locate all those involved with the process including sales, marketing, contracts, customer engineering, and customer services. And perhaps most important, a restructuring of all included functions around certain customers. In Nancy's words, "At the time, this was all huge and revolutionary."

Imagine the effort required to hold an appropriate and creative tension between the unique contributions of the individual members and the shared pursuit of results by the whole group. This is something of a "sweet spot" for extraordinary groups. To employ differences to their advantage, members need to believe that it is possible to grow from those differences; they then need to be willing to engage with each other so that new understandings can be gained. Then they will be ready to act. As we two know from our collaboration on this book this is not easy work. But it is essential to an extraordinary group experience.

Guidance for Preparing Yourself to Embrace Differences

Enhancing your ability to hold and build upon differences begins with what goes on inside you—how you feel about the differences you see and what you do because of them. You will be far more effective at helping your group be open to differences if you have found your own center first. What good is it to go into your group off-center or unbalanced, especially when it comes to issues that can inspire strong opinions and passionate debate? You will therefore notice that all of our questions and most of our actions in this section focus on what you could do alone or outside of group meetings. As with Chapters Four through Six, we encourage you to pick up your journal and take notes; follow through by applying some of the actions we highlight. By doing so, you will increase both your self-awareness and your skill.

Think about, write about, talk about, observe yourself with five suggestions in mind. Consider your willingness to

- Commit to your group
- Maintain a positive bias

- Be a learner and explorer
- Lean toward risk
- Provide less control and more space

Commit to Your Group

Consider your commitment to your group's Purpose and the people involved. The level of your commitment determines your willingness to openly explore the differences in your group. High commitment means you are capable of inspiring others and encouraging the group to capitalize on its diversity. Moderate commitment may build as the group gets under way, but depends on the level of commitment of others in the group. Low commitment is not likely to lead to an extraordinary experience; you won't have the focus and energy required and will have a harder time appreciating and learning from the group's diversity.

Reflection Questions for You.   Consider the importance you assign to your group's Purpose.

- How important is your group's Purpose to you? Why? What is your sense of how others in your group view the importance of your collective Purpose. What causes you to make this assessment?
- Consider your history with addressing differences in groups. Describe for yourself the roles and actions you have taken. What successful patterns do you see? What have you learned from those experiences that could be useful now?
- What risks are you willing to take to help this group have an extraordinary experience? What would you be willing to deny yourself for the sake of the group?

Sample Actions for You. Continue to reflect on your commitment to your group's Purpose through actions that push you into greater understanding.

- Describe what your group does when differences emerge. Particularly note any patterns in behavior and feelings expressed.

- Based on what you have read here, and your related thinking, list actions you are willing to take to promote your group's ability to embrace its differences. Picture yourself taking each those actions. Pick at least one and follow through with your group.

- Think of someone from your personal life who you care deeply about and with whom you also have differences. Identify an issue that exists between the two of you. Meet with that person with the intent of suspending your judgment and increasing your curiosity. Seek to understand that person's views more deeply. Make no decisions or judgments; just listen in order to better understand. After this conversation, take note of your experience and any insights you might have gained.

Maintain a Positive Bias

How would you increase the likelihood that your group could become exceptional if you operated from the belief that it will? If you aspire to be extraordinary in your group interactions, how might your behavior influence others? We encourage you to follow this line of questioning by operating from the assumption that your group could be amazing, fantastic, extraordinary! Since most of us go into groups with some kind of unconscious bias, choose a positive bias and see what happens as a result. Choose to see differences within your group as intriguing, informative, and essential to fulfilling the group's purpose. This mindset will help you see and build on the diversity of strengths other members bring. It will help you engage in disagreements as a learner—not as someone who already knows the "right" answer.

Reflection Questions for You. Go below the surface of some of your conscious patterns to examine the values or beliefs that influence your behavior.

- What is your "natural" bias toward organizations, work, and groups? How has that been evident to you and others? What does this suggest about developing a positive bias?

- What are times in your life when a positive bias paid off to your advantage? What did you gain because of this positive bias?

- If you were to act even more positively in group situations, what would that look like? What would you be doing that you are not now doing?

- What are the consequences for you of holding low expectations of the groups you are part of?

Sample Actions for You. Bring insight about your natural biases to your interaction with others in your life or in your group.

- Ask a friend or close family member about how they see your approach to work and groups. What do they pick up about your attitudes given what they hear you say or see you do? What effect does your approach have on what happens in the groups—as they see it?

- Make notes to yourself on what positive expectations could do for a particularly important group. Use those notes as a basis for what you say in your group.

- Go out of your way to know members of your group; find out about their backgrounds, training, experience, likes and dislikes. Share the same about yourself.

- Talk with group members about how you could better play off each other's strengths in order to advance your Purpose and increase your Impact.

Be a Learner and Explorer

The Group Needs model reminds us that individuals thrive in settings that help them learn and grow. Learning often comes when different viewpoints meet each other in a group discussion. Or learning can come if we take the first glimmers of confusion, frustration, or irritation as opportunities. Guide your thinking—and the group's—toward learning from the differences within the group. To do this, notice when you are about to judge another person wrong and declare yourself right. Replace your judgment with curiosity; get curious about other possibilities and open up to differing points of view. Behave in ways that show your respect for other perspectives and experiences, knowing that respect does not equal agreement. Actively seek information that will help you learn about another's opinion, what's behind it, its implications, and how it might support the group's Purpose.

Reflection Questions for You. Consider your patterns around judgment.

- What, if any, particular behaviors of others tend to push your hot-buttons? When your buttons get pushed and you slide toward judgment, how do you behave?

- What might you say or do to set aside your judge and reclaim your learner-explorer?

- Think of a time when your curiosity was fully engaged in a group. What enabled that to be so? Could you apply any of those factors in current situations in which you are inclined to judge rather than learn?

- What could you do to better demonstrate that you hear the views of others that are different from your own?

Sample Actions for You. These suggestions will help you become more conscious of your inclinations to judge or learn from others.

- Notice when your judging-self emerges in a group situation. How does that affect your ability to learn? What could you say in the group that would release some of your judgment?

- List phrases, statements, or questions that help you stay in the learner-explorer role. Examples: "Your point is that we need to. . . ." Or "I'd like to hear why you believe that is so important." Or "I've never thought of that." Refer to that list when you find yourself tempted to abandon the learner for the sake of your judge.

- List phrases, statements, or questions that suggest you are judging. For example, "We ought to. . ." Or "That's wrong." Or "I think we are done with this." Pay attention to how frequently such phrases make their way into your group interaction.

- Notice what allows you to accept the views of certain people and not others. How does this affect your group behavior? What might you do to accept more people? Is there any connection between what you have difficulty accepting in others and what you find hard to accept in yourself?

Lean Toward Risk

Extraordinary groups commonly talk about going places no one has gone before. Those we interviewed used words or phrases such as Nancy's "revolutionary" or "breakthrough" or "never been done before." Risk taking is always required in these circumstances. Keep in mind that when a group regularly chooses not to risk, nothing especially noteworthy is being aspired to or likely to happen. This is not horrible, but the chance that this will become a great group is significantly reduced.

Reflection Questions for You. Use these questions to gain insight about your willingness to undertake actions that carry risk.

- How would you describe yourself in terms of willingness to risk? What increases your willingness to risk?
- When has risking been particularly successful for you?
- What are some of the riskier elements of the work you do right now?
- What do your answers to the questions above suggest about how you want to approach the groups you are part of?

Sample Actions for You. Think about your group and the degree to which risk taking is necessary to become extraordinary.

- Remind yourself of your commitment to the group's Purpose. Describe a risk you would be willing to take to advance the group's Purpose.
- Assess yourself and your group against the indicators of extraordinary groups in Chapter Two. Which actions does your group commonly demonstrate? Which would

you like to get better at? Which actions seem particularly risky? Why might it be important to take that risk? What can you personally do to encourage others to take those risks?

- Assess your group's willingness to risk. Describe risky actions taken and readily supported. What else might the group do in the way of risk to make itself more effective? Ask others in your group what they see as useful but risky behavior.

Provide Less Control and More Space

Space to a group can mean the place it holds its meeting. But it can also refer to the psychological space—or safety—that is necessary to talk about differences. When people fear that talking about certain issues creates too much of a risk to take, they believe that moving into that conversation will result in some kind of reprisal or loss. They worry that "things will get out of hand" or "someone will get emotional!" With such feelings, they are less likely to make the space to talk about the issue at hand. At such moments, a desire to control the group or the conversation can ooze on to the scene. In extraordinary groups, members sense enough open and safe space for them to express their unique perspectives.

Consider your patterns of behavior in groups. How often do you want to be in control or do you avoid emotional encounters? If your answer is "much of the time," this may be a development opportunity for you. You've got plenty of company in these patterns, but less among members of extraordinary groups. If you want to help create an extraordinary group, behave as they behave. Support your group by encouraging it to find the space it needs for creative and passionate communication. Remind yourself of how amazing groups behave and be patient with your group when it moves in that direction, even if those behaviors cause you discomfort. Know that breakthrough thinking often comes from these more authentic and even chaotic moments. Support your group in loosening up rather than ratcheting down.

Reflection Questions for You. Give yourself permission to explore the question of control and how and when it might show up in your group behavior.

- Do you have tendencies to want to be right, to be first, to control, to avoid conflict or passionate interaction? If no, why not? If yes, why? How does any of these behaviors show up in your group meetings?
- What are the consequences of a group moving forward without your regular intervention to shape, manage, or control? What might happen in the extreme?
- Notice what your answers above suggest about the group's capabilities and your capabilities. How does this fit with your thoughts about you and your role in other groups? What clues, if any, do your answers offer about what you might do more or less of in the future?
- Think about your group and your commitment to its Purpose and its members. Ask yourself: How likely is it that my worries or fears will come true?

Sample Actions for You. Watch how the issues of space and control manifest themselves in your group.

- Notice yourself in your next group meeting. Do nothing differently except notice and note your reactions to what is going on. Notice when you find yourself wanting to be first, to be right, or to win. Ask yourself what you would do if you were more of a learner-explorer than a judger.

- Notice others in your next group meeting. Notice the more passionate members: How do they give voice to that passion? Where does it come from? How effective is it with others? How do others respond?

- Notice how much time or psychological space is provided in your group for exploring differences. What happens because it is there—or not? Make notes on the space available and how it is used and might be increased.

With these questions and actions, we complete our guidance on what you as an individual can do to prepare yourself to be more open to challenging differences in groups. That practice, mostly outside your group, prepares you well for stepping into the group to affect how it embraces its differences. And that is what the rest of this chapter is about.

Guidance for Encouraging Others to Embrace Differences

There is no lack of literature on interpersonal communication in group settings. A subset of that writing pays particular attention to conflict management; we strongly urge you to develop skills in this area. Pay particular attention to the writing that emphasizes, as we do, the opportunities embedded in diverse perspectives. There's no escaping the diversity of viewpoints in a group, so why not build upon them rather than pretend they will go away? From this point forward, we present and elaborate on three suggestions that increase a group's ability to hold differences:

- Model authentic communication.
- Meet Group Needs.
- Structure the group's work.

A quick clue before looking into Reflection Questions and Sample Actions in each of these three areas: it's all about modeling. By that we mean be the group member you want others to be. Do so with our three suggestions in mind. But more important, behave in ways that you truly believe will help join members of this group, make best use of its resources, and move it toward its desired outcomes. Over the long term, this is your best way to influence the group. You can begin today by emphasizing each of our three suggestions.

Model Authentic Communication

Openness and authenticity are about intention, not skills. You intend to fully engage, to be candid, forthright, and to be open to other points of view. And you intend that others in the group are this way too. This intention translates into behaviors such as clarifying your intent and asking others' about theirs; expressing what you want and asking others what they want; asking questions and paying attention to the answers; expressing how you feel and asking others how they feel; listening to learn and expecting others to listen too; being willing to change your mind and believing that others will do the same. All of which help embrace differences.

Do not worry about whether you are doing all of this perfectly. If you insist on worrying, worry more about whether all ideas have been heard so the group can act in an informed way. No, you don't have to express everything you think or feel, but do put relevant information on the table. Be honest, be clear, be respectful, be curious as you express yourself and encourage others to do the same. Authenticity is not a license to damage others or the group.

Reflection Questions for the Group. Invite your group members into a process of reflection about the level of candid communication in the group by asking these questions at an appropriate moment.

- As we work together, are we getting all the relevant thoughts and feelings on the table? What might we do to make that more likely?

- In service to our Purpose and the group itself, what are we more or less comfortable talking about together? What could we do to increase our comfort with a broader range of issues?

- When did we do a particularly good job of getting all our viewpoints expressed—even though they differed widely? What allowed that to work? How could we do more of that?

Sample Actions in the Group. Here are some more detailed actions related to the authenticity in your group; they compliment the reflection questions above.

- When disagreement emerges in the group, ask the parties involved to clarify their intentions as they put forth their ideas. Ask the group how the intentions are similar and different. Summarize what they have in common; see what happens next.

- When you find yourself confused about what is going on in the group, say, "I'm feeling confused . . . Where are we going with this conversation? Can anyone help me out?"

Your candor is likely to call out others having a similar experience and the group can adapt to this.

- When you find yourself worrying what you see going on in the group, say aloud what you are worried about. Again, your willingness to name your concerns will help others do the same. Once out, these feelings will help the group make a conscious decision about how to proceed.

- When your commitment is high, tell the group your feelings. Similarly, if you are particularly pleased to be able work with others in the group, let them know that individually and collectively—along with your reasons.

Meet Group Needs

As your group deals with its differences, consider the Group Needs model as it applies to each person in the group. Notice how the creative dynamic among the six can surface as conflicts or paradoxes:

- A person is highly committed to the group's identity (Bond and Purpose) and loves to shine individually (Acceptance and Potential) by representing the group to the community at large.

- Another member is committed to the mission of the group (Purpose and Impact) but is frightened by what he might be called upon to do (Acceptance and Potential) along the way.

- Someone usually shy about speaking up in group meetings (Acceptance and Bond) contributes enthusiastically when the group is at work (Purpose and Impact).

- A member aggressively asserts opinions to influence the group direction (Acceptance and Purpose) but does so in a way that causes others to distance themselves (Bond).

When you see the Group Needs being expressed by some-one, think first about how you might help meet those needs. Even when tempted to pull away, recognize this person has a real need and that backing off does not meet that need. When you hear someone say something that indicates she might be looking for validation and support, say, "I support you" if you do. If you don't agree with her views, paraphrase what she has said so that she knows you have understood her position. When you think someone does not feel included, include them by name in what you say. When someone is going on and on about what the group is supposed to do, tell him you appreciate his commitment to this group.

It's amazing how effective small actions like these can be. Use your needs-oriented view to get beneath what was said; help everyone hear the Group Needs as they are expressed. When you hear and make relevant the hopes, concerns, or needs of group members, you nudge your group toward excellence.

Reflection Questions for the Group. Help your group be more responsive to the six Group Needs that members bring by posing these questions and encouraging discussion about the answers.

- After listening to all we've said, what do you think this group needs most right now? How much of this is about what we want individually or what we want together as a group? About what we do or how we do it? How do we make sure all of our needs are being addressed as we work together?

- What can we do in this group to help each of us bring our energies to the group, to connect with our Purpose and each other, to make us more hopeful about what we can do in the world?

- Do our needs conflict in any way? If so, how? Do we want or need to do anything about this conflict?

Sample Actions in the Group. Think about the Group Needs model as a powerful template to recognize what other members are expressing and then do your part to meet those needs. Here are some ways you can use it with any of your groups.

- Put the Group Needs model before the group on a flip chart or white board. Around the sides list examples of the needs that are met in your group's experience. Ask what else might be done to meet more Group Needs more often. List those ideas and through discussion determine which are most important. Ask how the group might accomplish these things together in meetings. Make commitments to move ahead.
- When you see the group drifting, arguing, seeming disjointed, ask: What is going on right now? Hear responses and then ask: What could we do that would meet more of our collective needs?
- Ask group members to read Chapters Four, Five, and Six before an upcoming meeting. In the meeting, ask: Which Group Needs seem most prevalent in this group? How do we meet them now? How might we better meet them?

Structure the Group's Work

People behave differently when asked to work within a new framework, and this can be especially useful when encouraging others to embrace differences. By "structure" we mean shaping the context within which work is done. That includes altering the place the work is done; the design within which people

work; the roles people play while they work; the ground rules they follow as they work. Alter any of these elements and people behave differently. Apply these suggestions about structuring in the spirit of just-enough rather than too much structure. Do so in order to help members be more open to group differences.

Location. Take a group out of its accustomed place of work and members immediately start behaving differently; this is one reason for the popularity of group retreats. Attend to the aesthetics of the meeting space; how can it be made more attractive and inviting? Getting out of the office for a picnic or business-related trip can help members discover their shared humanity and learn about each other on a personal as well as work basis. Shared experiences in a comfortable setting place member's differences in larger perspective. Meeting in a new setting supports creating new options.

Meeting Designs. Long-established groups become accustomed to their meeting formats and agendas, all of which can produce a giant and silent yawn. Designing a meeting differently energizes the group and mixes their talents anew; a good design can cause everyone to learn about others in new ways that increase the creativity of the group and allow appreciation of differences. It can be as simple as focusing an entire meeting on all that has made the group successful; or bringing in a provocative speaker and then having a discussion about her ideas; or picking a recent challenging situation and debriefing it together to mine the lessons-learned. We offer additional thoughts about meeting design in Chapter Nine.

Roles. Just as we become accustomed to the format of our meetings, so we become accustomed to the roles each group member plays. Shifting roles shifts perspectives, often reducing

conflict as people better understand what is expected of others. For example, when leadership of group meetings is shared, rather than constantly held by one person. Or when everyone in the group is expected to think and act as one leader among many in the group. Or asking one or two people to observe the meeting dynamics and report back their observations to spark a discussion near the close of the meeting. Or sharing the responsibility for taking and distributing meeting notes.

Ground Rules. Groups work within explicit and implicit rules; members think they all know what the rules are—even though they may each express the rules differently when asked. Ground rules have huge impact. For example, imagine a simple ground rule that says, "We will hear from each member before making group decisions." For many groups, that would open up a whole new way of working. This is not to recommend establishing particular ground rules necessarily, but to emphasize the impact of relevant ground rules. Think about the potential of ground rules for managing differences and embracing disagreement. All groups have such agreements, whether they know it or not. Extraordinary groups are more explicit about what norms they need in order to succeed. This includes ground rules that encourage differences to surface and be explored.

Reflection Questions for the Group. Help your group think about the way it can be more intentional about location, meeting design, roles, and ground rules so that different perspectives are encouraged.

- How does the physical location we meet in positively or negatively affect how we interact and our intended outcomes? What other locations might also work for us, and how might they affect our outcomes?

- How does the structure of our regular meetings affect what we accomplish? What alternative structure would enable a wider range of ideas to come forward and energize us?

- How could we shake up the roles we perform in a way that results in more creativity, excitement, and learning?

- What are our implied rules that allow us to be so effective? And what rules block our work together? What rules do we need in order to help us be more open and curious?

Sample Actions in the Group. Build upon the insights gained from group reflection by changing some of your structure so that you can more effectively engage around your differences.

- Together assess your regular group meetings, their effectiveness for the group and for individuals in the group— within the context of your Purpose and desired Impact. Particularly attend to what the group does to call ideas forth, to put an array of ideas beside each other, to decide what to do with all the group has learned.

- Look at the way your group "always" goes about doing whatever it does. For patterns that seem entrenched, suggest doing them differently. For example, consider changing the order of the standing items on your agenda, rotating the responsibilities for facilitating your meetings. Try changing seats if certain people always sit in the same place. Discuss how such changes impact the group.

- After successfully facing unexpected adversity, look at what you did together to address this unplanned, emergent issue. Use your next meeting to properly celebrate, taking time to honor people's contributions and efforts. Talk about what you've learned, what you'd like to forget, and how this experience served the group.

- Meet in a new place, a place that most agree is likely to work but is still significantly different from the "old place." It may be a room with a view or a coffee shop or someone's home, but new it is and it will make a difference. Try including a meal; food has a remarkable communal effect on groups. Discuss how this variation encouraged openness and the ability to work with differences.

For your review, one more time, here are the eight suggestions to help you and your group engage fully and even joyfully with one another around your exciting, provocative, intriguing, thought-provoking, and powerful differences.

- Commit to your group.
- Maintain a positive bias.
- Be a learner and explorer.
- Lean toward risk.
- Provide less control and more space.
- Model authentic communication.
- Meet Group Needs.
- Structure the group's work.

Embracing differences has particular meaning for us as your co-authors. During our three-year collaboration, we gradually developed and then intentionally applied each of the above suggestions. Our experience influenced what we have written here. See Appendix C, in which we describe how our small group of two went about embracing our differences while writing this book. Since many group collaborations are a collection of one-on-one interactions, you might find our lists helpful.

9

LEADING EXTRAORDINARY GROUPS

In this chapter, we focus our guidance, reflection questions, and sample actions on the role of the group leader. If you are a facilitator of groups, our ideas offer good guidance on approaching your role with our model in mind. If you are a group member, remember that the extraordinary groups we studied were characterized by shared leadership. In the best examples, everyone in the group initiated as a leader might initiate, offered ideas as a leader might, and proposed actions—more in the mode of an active leader than a passive member. Our suggestions offer a look into some of the less visible aspects of exceptional groups. Whatever your role, we assume that you aspire to the extraordinary and that you intend to take action to encourage amazing group experiences. Every suggestion in this chapter is designed to help you to do just that.

We focus on six leadership actions that directly encourage the eight indicators of amazing groups we identified in Chapter Two: a compelling purpose, shared leadership, just-enough structure, full engagement, embracing differences, unexpected learning, strengthened relationships, and great results. Each suggestion promotes group activity that can lead to an experience in which people feel energized, connected, hopeful, and changed. If you want, through your leadership, to help your group be extraordinary, pay particular attention to our suggestions. For some readers, our guidance will be welcome reminders; for others, it will open up new territory.

We pull from the experiences reported to us through our field study and our own experiences in the last three years as we deliberately applied the Group Needs model to our consulting work. We intentionally do not address many important and basic aspects of effective group leadership; these topics are well covered by many other authors; check our list of valued references in Appendix D to learn more.

Group Leadership

Half of the transformational groups we learned about had someone designated with a title such as "team lead" or "department head" or "project manager." Regardless of title, that person's leadership was expected and important to the group's success. Group leaders feel responsible for outcomes and direction of a group. In large organizations, especially workplaces, they are typically assigned that responsibility. Self-organizing groups create their own process for identifying leaders sometimes resulting in one person being elected, named, or annointed as the leader. Regardless of how they come to their position of leader, they usually have experience, knowledge, and relationships important to the group's Purpose and the world in which the group operates. They expect people will turn to them for some level of direction, guidance, and encouragement. In extraordinary groups, they seek full engagement of all members and encourage others to think and act as leaders too.

Facilitative Leadership

We found that leaders of extraordinary groups most often employ a style that is more facilitative than directive. Facilitative leaders focus on being of service to the group as a whole and to individual members. They attend to how the group works together as it progresses toward outcomes. They see to it that the group gets the direction it needs without necessarily providing all that direction themselves. They act out of the belief that their group must share responsibility, accountability, participation, and power.

The choice to be a facilitative leader is enabled by seeing through the lens of the Group Needs model. Stand back from your group to consider the individual members, their collective Purpose, and the world in which they operate. From that larger perspective, consider the six Group Needs brought by every member: How might this group experience meet those needs? Next, consider the eight indicators of extraordinary groups discussed in Chapter Two: Are those indicators alive in your meetings? And notice whether members exhibit the four feelings associated with transformation: Do they seem energized, hopeful, connected—and positively changed? Answering these questions helps you lead in ways that call forth the strengths and motivations of your group.

Guidance for Leaders

To create an extraordinary group experience, consider this guidance—all rooted in the designated leader role, all designed with the Group Needs model in mind:

- Frame an inspiring Purpose.
- Lead with a light touch.
- Keep issues discussable.
- Manage the world around your group.
- Put the right team together.
- Design and facilitate meetings with the Group Needs in mind.

Frame an Inspiring Purpose

Members are inspired when they find meaning or significance in a group's Purpose. An important early-on action is to help group members discover this personal connection. In doing so, you are essentially asking members to consider such questions as: Why is this Purpose important to you? What about it causes you to be highly committed to the work of our group? Some groups come to this understanding once a project is under way. Other groups begin with a boldly stated Purpose, in which the larger meaning is abundantly clear. Take a look at Dan's experience.

Naming the Larger Impact. Dan was asked to lead a team in developing the security component for an important piece of new software. Because of the intended widespread use of this particular product, he framed the work as "securing civilization." He admits that "At first it sounded a bit corny," but the larger meaning of the work caught on. "This rallied the team and they lived it. Every day, they had a chance to make a difference. This upped the quality bar tremendously." Having framed the Purpose in this broad and inspiring way, his team set and met their aggressive targets for building and testing security features. From the beginning, Dan saw the meaning of the work and captured it in a phrase that conveyed a huge and inspiring Impact. Throughout the effort, he would remind team members of the significance of what they had taken on together and why it was important for each team member to make this work a priority. This hugely motivational element contributed to an outstanding success: All the quality bars were hit, no deadlines were missed, and a remarkably low number of fixes were required once the product was released. Dan's framing of the Purpose was key.

The "aggressive targets" of Dan's group points to another powerful action leaders can take that is related to framing an inspiring Purpose. If you lead a group with an external-change Purpose, help the group set doable stretch goals. These statements will focus the group's action and translate the compelling Purpose into the concrete accomplishments that help a group go from point A to point B—and achieve unexpected learning along the way. Among our field study stories, compelling Purpose and doable stretch goals were the most frequently mentioned examples of structure.

Reflection Questions for the Leader. These questions will help you reflect on how your group's Purpose inspires, is expressed, and can be linked to stretch goals.

- What is your group's Purpose? How clear is it to the group? How does it inspire you?

- What larger individual, group, or world needs might be found within the presenting Purpose? How might those be expressed?

- What can you uniquely do from your position to help group members find inspiration or personal connection with the group's Purpose? How might you involve members in deepening the meaning of their Purpose?

- What stretch goals will lead to the accomplishment of this Purpose? How might you involve the group in identifying and shaping those goal statements?

Notice that these questions are useful to group members and facilitators as well as leaders. This will be true of all of the reflection questions and many of the sample actions offered throughout this chapter.

Sample Actions with Groups. Help group members find personal inspiration in the group's Purpose through the following actions.

- Ask group members to share their thoughts about the group's Purpose by posing such questions as: What does our Purpose mean to you? What greater Impact do you see within it? Why is our Purpose important to you? How will the power of this Purpose influence your participation?

- If it is not clearly defined already, ask two or three members of the group to draft the group's current Purpose for review at the next group meeting. Encourage a discussion using the questions mentioned above. Notice how members are aligned or not around Purpose. Does the degree of alignment suggest any next steps the group should take?

- After you and the group have explored the larger meaning of your Purpose, define the goals that will enable you to fulfill it. Examine the draft statements with this question: Are these goals challenging yet doable, and will they cause us to stretch our capabilities—as individuals? As a group?

Lead with a Light Touch

Amazing groups create space for people to think creatively, explore tangents, have fun, take risks, do integrative thinking, and build connections with one another. Members of such groups are passionate about Purpose and focused on challenging goals. Such groups do not do well with tightly structured agendas, roles, boundaries, or micro-managing. These traditional management techniques create structure that blocks the energy and sense of connection.

With your groups, strive for just-enough structure to create clarity for members and support their commitment to Purpose. This openness joins with the another important aspect of leadership—using a low-keyed style that is much more behind the scenes than out front. Leaders of transformational groups understand that the leadership they provide is not about themselves, but rather about how they encourage and support the group members to fulfill the group's Purpose. If you want your groups to be extraordinary, do not try to control them. Open up the group's structure and process—and open up yourself—to see what emerges from the group. This lighter-touch, adaptive leadership is all about creating space for others to jump in, being present for support, listening and watching carefully, and coaching members as they take on more responsibility. Be careful when you feel inclined to reinforce boundaries, structure, or the power of your role. Instead, use your leadership to focus the group on the outcomes desired. Control rarely and only when necessary to support the group's ability to move ahead. Consider Marcia's leadership.

A Cultural Reconnection. Like many other of the leaders we interviewed, Marcia had no idea what she was unleashing when she led a cultural reconnection mission of nineteen African American women to Kenya. Now, seven years later, Marcia is one of many group member-leaders of the thriving nonprofit organization that emerged from that first trip. These life-changing trips continue with the support of the organization's Vision and Planning Team, essentially the leadership circle. When asked about her evolving leadership role, Marcia says, "My role now is to step back. I make sure I'm supporting the Vision and Planning Team members in their personal and professional lives." She describes the women in this core group as "powerhouses in their own rights," many of whom are well known in their communities. "In some ways, they are isolated due to the power and positions they have. Here, it is different. They are on a par with one another. They want to make sure they are contributing in a way that matches who they are."

With such strong members, any attempt on Marcia's part to control the group would be counter productive. In the spirit of light-touch leadership, she adds, "I have been careful not to take on any one job on my own. I am trying to affirm them in their roles and be present when it is strategic for me to be there. Now this group runs on its own energy." When asked about her unique contribution as the group's founder, she knows she has an important leadership role to play: "I look after the whole group, listening for where we are at. No one else plays this role. Affirmation is everything. We must continuously affirm and thank each other. Our success is based on collective action, and so I've relinquished everything to the group."

Reflection Questions for the Leader. Use this set of questions to think about your leadership style.

- How would you describe yourself as a leader in terms of the lightness-to-heaviness of your style? Give some examples.
- How does leading with a light touch suit you? What might be the consequences of this style for you? For group members?
- What might you do to lighten-up to benefit the group and its Purpose?

Sample Actions with the Group. These suggestions will help you address issues related to control, structure, and the support you provide to group members.

- Think about how you have been leading lately. When did you do things that represented a desire to take control? When did you do things that modeled leading with a light touch? For each situation, identify someone who was present and ask that person for feedback about the impact of your actions.

- Consider the boundaries and structure your group works within. How tightly constrained do members feel by these boundaries? Ask members about the structure of their work and how elements of this structure help or hinder them as they do their work. Identify and make necessary changes.

- Ask the group to reflect on how leadership surfaces in the group: What do people do to help lead this group? Are there patterns in this shared leadership? In the context of this discussion, ask for feedback on your own leadership. Are there things you could do differently to promote a higher degree of shared leadership?

Keep Issues Discussable

Diverse views, skills, and backgrounds often produce a heady concoction of both passionate agreement and disagreement. We focused on the tension between the strength and challenge of such differences in the previous chapter. Leaders of extraordinary groups create a safe place for people to express and embrace their differences. Look for opportunities to air the opinions of members. Help them get below the surface to identify lurking issues they hesitate to bring up. Model openness to and curiosity about issues when they are raised. In doing so, you make it safe for members to raise concerns, talk about their fears, challenge the status quo, offer tough feedback, make passionate speeches, share personal experiences, and call out mixed messages.

All of these behaviors—while sometimes not politically correct or comfortable—are essential for a group of individuals to authentically engage with one another and call forth important information, issues, and opinions. These moments of authentic-but-uncomfortable conversation were often reported to us as those that are long remembered as the catalytic event that transformed a group. Reinforce the value of seeing the whole by keeping potentially contentious issues on the table and open for discussion. As you do so, encourage members to listen to and learn from one another. Consider Jane's group and her leadership.

Clinical Research in Uncharted Waters. Jane recalled a complex research project she led for her company—a large national consulting firm specializing in supply chain management in health care. Her team of seven designed a product evaluation process for surgical instruments from multiple vendors. They initiated this research in order to determine which products would best meet customer requirements. Prior to this point, no objective comprehensive evaluation—involving practicing surgeons—had ever been done with this category of instruments. We were able to interview Jane and three of her group's members. This professionally diverse group "left behind different and specialized clinical backgrounds and became learners together"—and faced many challenges. "We had a clear mission to produce a success in a project that none of us had ever done before. We were in uncharted waters with a restricted budget and a project whose details could not be discussed with others in the company—outside of our group—for fear of destroying the project integrity." In the

end, they successfully tested equipment in twenty-one sur-
geries at major university medical schools in six different
states.

Jane is an experienced leader who pays equal attention
to outcomes and relationships among team members. Still,
at times members were "cynical, argumentative, or depressed
and had to talk through issues." This ability—to talk about
what needed to be talked about, even if it was difficult—
was a core competency that Jane intentionally established
and encouraged within the group. It was in place before the
most demanding part of the project arrived. The benefits
of this competence, described by one member as "trust in
the group"—were clear to all: "With respect for each other
and courage, we stormed, normed, and then performed at
high levels. And, in the end, we did do what we set out
to do!"

Reflection Questions for the Leader. Consider how your
group deals with undiscussable issues.

- When your group is faced with tough issues and makes
  them discussable, what does the group do? What do you
  do that supports this?
- When your group has difficulty facing an important yet
  undiscussable issue, what does it do to avoid the issue?
  Why does it do this? What are the concerns? And, how
  do you react?
- What might you do or say that would model openness
  and a willingness to open up subjects that seem taboo or
  fraught with difficulty?

Sample Actions for the Group. Encourage more open conversations in your group through these actions.

- When you sense that someone is hesitating to bring up a risky subject, encourage that member to be more specific by paraphrasing what you hear, asking for an example, expressing your desire to hear more.

- After a great discussion filled with candor, passion, and increased understanding, ask members to reflect on their experiences with questions such as: How was this conversation risky? What are your observations about how we interacted? What impact do conversations like this have on how we work together?

- Ask each member to write down his or her answers to this question: What helps you to feel safe enough in this group to bring up a risky subject? Ask each person to offer a suggestion; build a list that everyone can see. Discuss the items and make appropriate modifications, then ask: How can we use this guidance? Discuss, decide, and follow through.

Manage the World Around Your Group

Most groups operate within a larger workplace, community, or culture. When people in those larger organizations think about who is responsible for your group, they think of you. When your group members think about who represents them to the larger organization or community, they also think of you. You become the radar, constantly scanning the environment for realities in your world that might aid or block your group's work, specifically the organizational support, resources, information, and context your group will need in order to do its work. And your radar is also at work inside the group as you scan for how it is doing, how you represent it to the world around you. In particularly political environments, you act as a buffer between the larger arena and your group, protecting them from outside dynamics that can distract or discourage them while giving them an internal place to "let off steam" in ways that do not damage the group in the organization.

Return to Jane's Group. As her group's leader, Jane was the person to interface with her organization on behalf of her team. Her job was complicated by the fact that she really couldn't talk about the details of the project. She had to maintain strict silence about the research process in order to protect against any possible perception of organizational bias related to the eventual findings. When it came to the budget, Jane remembers that she was "always tin-cupping the dollars." Many of the company's senior leaders "came from the for-profit perspective and were not used to relying on clinical or academic expertise." Many people were skeptical because they knew the group would have to work in academic settings. She comments that "there was a strong desire to control" what her team was doing because of "the heavy-duty expectations as to what would happen as a result of our research."

Any of these realities could have blocked or complicated her group's ability to succeed. Jane's job was to work the intersection between her group and others in her company—others who might look at, wonder about, try to influence or question the group and its work. She secured funds, resisted pressure to influence the project, and brought in necessary resources. Fortunately, Jane had solid relationships with senior staff in her company, political savvy, and well-developed communications and negotiating skills. Even so, she recalls that to manage these communications appropriately, "I constructed likely questions and answers about the project and vetted them with the team. Staying on script was often not easy, but they were counting on me to be their scout, their early warning system, and their protector so that our important work could be done." Although her story contained more complications than many, when it comes to this aspect of leading a group you will be well served if you develop strengths similar to Jane's.

Reflection Questions for the Leader. Think about yourself as the "radar", the go-between or the point-person that works the space in between your group and the context in which it operates.

- When you think about the world around your team, what forces, organizations, or individuals come to mind as being most important to deal with—ones that could block or aid your group and its Purpose?
- What abilities do you need as a leader to deal with the forces that have an impact on your group? How do you assess your present abilities in relation to what you need?
- What is your reaction to carrying the responsibility of dealing with your group's world in order to make it more successful? How much does this attract or repel you? What are the implications of your answers for working in that outer world?

Sample Actions with Groups. With your group, identify the political or influence issues that will affect the work you have come together to do.

- With your group, chart the significant individuals, departments, or groups that affect your group and its Purpose. Make it visual so that members can understand and work with items on the list.
- Identify the most significant forces in your surrounding world—the forces that deserve attention, caution, or

action. Note which forces you can control, those you can influence, and those you cannot control or influence. Consider how to best deal with each of these forces.

- Decide what actions your group needs to take toward influencing the surrounding world and who should take those actions. Make sure you follow through on actions that you, as the leader, should take; report back to your group to let them know the results.

Put the Right Team Together

Amazing groups do not require people who have elevated levels of interpersonal insight or fabulous communication skills. But they do require that collectively members possess enough of the knowledge, skills, or experience to tackle the group's Purpose. Perhaps even more important, members must be committed enough to the group's Purpose so that they are willing to set aside self-interests for the good of the whole. As a leader, you may play a pivotal role in inviting members to join the group or encouraging other members to share this responsibility. Either way, pay attention to why each member joins. Behave in ways that encourage members' Acceptance and Potential and nurture the group Bond. When members sense that these three Group Needs are attended to, their commitment to Purpose will increase. As it does, they will be better able and more willing to embrace differences and put the group's Purpose and Impact first.

Bringing the right people together is critical in group formation, but sometimes it does not work. When a member's values or style repeatedly conflict with or undercut the group's collaborative spirit or its commitment to Purpose, you may need to help that person leave the group. Often this person puts self-interest first, the group Purpose second, and the success and well-being of other members last. These self-serving behaviors are particularly damaging when the person possesses critical skills, or when the individual manipulates others.

A leader can be slow to pick up on the pattern of misalignment and be reluctant to lose someone with valuable skills or knowledge. Collaborative leaders often hesitate to judge a contrary approach as unacceptable; they try to bring this member "back into the fold." But such members sow seeds of confusion, mistrust, and frustration. When it occurs, it needs to be addressed quickly and respectfully so the group stays on track. In self-organizing groups, this responsibility can be shared. But when you represent the hierarchy to your group, this difficult task will probably be yours. In all of this, you are likely to end up having direct and confrontational conversations about the member's behavior, its impact on others, why this is unacceptable, and the need for his or her departure from the group. Fortify yourself with the knowledge that the culture, the momentum, and the success of your group is at stake.

Return to Dan's Group. Dan faced such a circumstance. One of the members of his leadership team, Frank, had an edge—a competitive manner that surfaced periodically and then became more pointed and counterproductive by frequently asking for more staff, suggesting that production problems in his area were actually caused by others on Dan's team, finally giving his staff direction to do things that were contrary to Dan's plan because "Dan really doesn't understand the issues." Dan referenced his challenge with Frank when asked about the three factors that enabled his group experience to be so powerful. One of his points was "putting the right team together." Moving Frank out "made a huge difference. We accomplished twice as much after he left. This gave me the ability to build a management team that had the values of the organization and different skill sets, creating what we wanted for the whole team."

Dan wanted his direct reports to be solid leaders "who would say what was on their minds, challenge each other, and be there for each other." When Frank was in the mix, the other group members were constantly on guard, watching for what Frank might do next to stir the pot. The reality Dan eventually faced was that there was no way he could get the level of trust, collaboration, and cross-functional innovation he needed while Frank was still a member of the group. He had to take action in order to protect his team and its ability to fulfill its Purpose.

Reflection Questions for the Leader. Use these questions to help you gain insight about the challenge of getting the right people on your team.

- In your experience with successful groups, what are the key elements beyond technical competence needed to form and keep a group together through time? How does your current group fit with your past successful experience?
- What are the indicators that you currently have the right talents, experience, motivations, and individuals in place? What else do you need? What are you doing to further develop the talent already in the group?
- What experience do you have in removing a person from a team? If you had to do it again, how would you approach it? To whom would you turn for advice and support?

Sample Actions for a Group. Engage your group in conversation that highlights collective capabilities and commitment.

- Ask the group to assess the capabilities (technical skills, knowledge, experience, relationships, industry knowledge, connections, interpersonal skills, motivation) needed to fully realize its Purpose and desired Impact.

- With that assessment in mind, encourage group members to identify the ways in which their own capabilities—or those they see in other group members—match what is needed. Consider the implications of this list: Do additional capabilities need to be developed or brought in? Do current plans and roles enable members to apply their full capabilities?

- Look for ways to support members' personal and professional development through the group activities or assignments. Pause periodically to appreciate the contributions of members and acknowledge the development of members through their work in the group.

Design and Facilitate Meetings with the Group Needs in Mind

In order to be a group, people must meet. Face-to-face or through technology, people come together to fulfill their shared Purpose. As you design and lead your meetings, intentionally apply the Group Needs model. Doing so will increase the likelihood that your meetings will engage group members and focus their interaction in ways that are personally satisfying and productive.

In designing your meetings, consider both the topics for the agenda and the process you will use to address those topics. Ask yourself five questions:

- How will this meeting meet the needs of Acceptance and Potential, Bond and Purpose, Reality and Impact?

- Where and how can we use our differences as a group strength?

- Does this meeting have just-enough structure to create focus but not so much as to block members' creative thinking, full engagement, and honest conversation?

- Is there enough room in the agenda so that members have the time for these more in-depth and sometimes complex conversations?

- What approaches will maximize the full engagement of all members and shared leadership?

When a group meets on a regular basis, it's not necessary for each meeting to attend to each of the six Group Needs. However, over time strive to touch each of these needs. In each meeting, find ways to tap differences as a strength and to employ the notion of just-enough structure. By doing so, you will consistently reinforce the value of diverse perspectives, creativity, candor, and member accountability for the group's success. Of course, if you are planning a one-meeting event, do your best to manifest as many of the Group Needs as possible.

When leading the meeting, do so in a facilitative style that moves the process along and actively engages members. Use more questions than statements; be willing to offer your observations—not judgments—about the group's process. Monitor the amount of time that you are the one speaking. Typically, the amount of "air time" you take should be less than other members of the group; members will see you as more facilitative than directive when the bulk of what you say is focused on the group's process and not your opinions about any particular subject. Rely on your good listening skills to paraphrase and clarify members' comments when needed—especially when differences start to surface. From time to time, you will no doubt feel the need to "put on your leader hat." These will be moments when you might need to set or clarify direction, share a broader view, or make a decision. When you do so, call out this shift. This clarification will be useful to group members and be a good reminder to yourself to move back into the facilitator mode as quickly as possible.

Through all of this, look for ways to encourage Acceptance and Potential, Bond and Purpose, Reality and Impact. If you are fortunate enough to partner with a group facilitator, make sure that that person understands the Group Needs model. Together talk about how you can both be on the look-out for ways to reinforce the six Group Needs. Rely on your facilitator to take the lead around meeting design and facilitation. But make sure you are involved in setting the outcomes for each meeting and agree on the approach to use for various portions of the agenda. At the end of each meeting, take time to debrief together, so that you can learn from your experience and make plans for how to move ahead.

Reflection Questions for the Leader. Think through your answers to these questions to help design your meetings and prepare to lead them in a facilitative manner.

- How would a meeting design based on the Group Needs model differ from what you would typically do? What benefits would come from this?
- What is most important for the group to accomplish in this meeting? What do those outcomes have to do with underlying Group Needs as expressed in the model?
- What have you done to make it more likely that your questions and observations are welcome in the group? Will the group be surprised by a facilitative way of leading?

Sample Actions with the Group. Use these suggestions to bring the power of the Group Needs model into your group meetings.

- As you design your agendas, consider using the language of the six Group Needs. For example: Defining our Reality. Understanding our Purpose. Creating our connection or Bond. Anticipate opportunities to ask questions that reflect some of the Group Needs. For example: What are we learning? How do we tap each other's strengths? A year from now, what Impact will we be proud to have achieved?

- Gather data ahead of time from each individual in the group. Among your questions, ask what they need from this group. Or ask: What would this group have to do to be truly extraordinary? Present what you learn at the meeting.

- At the beginning of the group, say that you want this experience to be extraordinary—a group that will be highly productive and an experience that people will look back on with great excitement and appreciation. Say why this is important to you.

- Describe your intention to lead in a facilitative way. Ask the group to discuss when they think your explicit and more directive leadership is particularly important. Use this discussion to propose what you intend to do. Be clear about your agreements with the group and stick with them.

- As you watch the group, look for examples of the eight indicators of amazing groups or the four feelings of transformation or the six Group Needs being satisfied. Ask for group members' observations or offer your own.

A simple question such as "What just happened?" can trigger an important recognition of extraordinary group dynamics. Appendix B may be a useful tool for you.

In this chapter we have presented six leadership suggestions:

- Frame an inspiring Purpose.
- Lead with a light touch.
- Keep issues discussable.
- Manage the world around your group.
- Put the right team together.
- Design and facilitate meetings with the Group Needs in mind.

We offer this platform on which you can build your own group leadership strategies.

So what results from the type of leadership we have described in this chapter? Given what we've learned from our interviews and the extraordinary groups we've been blessed to be a part of, here's what it can look like.

You may find yourself with a group in which it is sometimes difficult to keep up with the shifting roles, and members adapt to what a moment calls for in the shared quest for accomplishment. As the group leader, you step forward then back, having posed a question that provokes an enlivened discussion in which nobody seems to be in charge but everyone knows what they are working on. In this moment a younger group member makes an impassioned plea. You turn that plea into a question. And now everybody is going at it once again, until someone asks for quiet and proposes a step forward. Now everyone is jumping on that, but the proposer persists and asks people to declare where they stand. You are actively engaged in listening but resist the temptation to try to control or organize what is happening. People's declarations produce yet another proposal from another member, which builds on the last but captures wider support. Now you test the will of the group on this suggestion; members agree, and identify next steps and accountabilities. You look around the room and see people leaning forward; others are smiling; some look relieved. The feelings of energy, connection, hope, and change are alive in the room.

That's what one extraordinary group looks like! *That's* what it feels like! And *that's* what can be accomplished by a facilitative leader intent on creating an extraordinary group!

10

LIVING THE PROMISE OF EXTRAORDINARY GROUPS

During the three years on the path to completing this book, our learning has been immense! Very little of the book you hold was in the first or second draft. Our journey began with a desire to move beyond our mostly successful but less satisfying work with groups. We suspected there was something more and didn't know what it was. We loved the idea of a shared exploration, not knowing our destination. And, so far, we have reached here: One model, six needs, eight indicators, four feelings, and twenty-six suggestions. Progress? Certainly! End of story? Not a chance! We pause on this challenging, frustrating, and exhilarating journey to offer a handful of thoughts especially important to us—and perhaps to you.

Small Groups Hold Huge Potential

Increasingly, complex problems or opportunities will require the attention of small groups because no one person has the capacity to address such issues alone. At work, in our communities, in our families, with our friends, we will continue to join in various clusters to get something done or to support each other's endeavors. Technology will further connect us in ways we cannot yet imagine and continue the reshaping of our world. The explosion of online educational programs and second-life experiences remind us of an observation from our field study—people in virtual groups have basically the same needs as those in who meet face-to-face. Those of Generation Y—those tens of millions born between 1976 and 2000—have grown up on technology and are making virtual groups even more common. These virtual connections will leap over distance, time, languages, and cultures to join us in new ways.

People Need Groups and Extraordinary Groups Meet Their Needs

These twin truths are critical to all we've learned. We humans know in our bones our dependence on each other; we have known that for millennia upon millennia. We will seek out groups to belong to and bond with whether the prevailing structure wants us to or not. When we experience a group as extraordinary, we are experiencing the meeting of deep set human needs we have especially for groups.

Our ideas about small groups also apply to groups larger than twenty, but there is a point where the creative magic runs out. Let's not fool ourselves about the consequences of piling dozens or hundreds of people into one organization. It can do a lot, but it is not likely to amaze us in how it meets people's needs. No other structure besides a small group—especially no larger, hierarchical structure—is capable of consistently providing the fulfillment each of us seeks through the company of others.

Creating amazing group experiences is about meeting those core human needs of Acceptance and Potential, Bond and Purpose, Reality and Impact. When we understand these Group Needs, we can begin to act—for our own benefit and to support others. Regardless of role—member, leader, or facilitator—and armed with this insight, we can act first to help meet the needs brought by others. And then to be ready to have our own needs met as others take similar action.

Extraordinary Group Experiences can Appear Quite Ordinary

We were surprised to discover early on that most people had a wonderful group experience they would love to share with us. The extraordinary was more ordinary than we had imagined! The extraordinary is not delivered, wrapped in the cover of *Fortune*, *Fast Company*, or the Harvard *Business Review*. It does not require graduate degrees in group process skills or leadership. It is happening around us, among regular folks who have had delightful group experiences they would like to repeat again and again. People coming from vastly different circumstances spoke to remarkably similar patterns. Each understood the special, unforgettable quality of something amazing that happened with others. And while some would just as soon leave behind their grim situations or the burnout that came from long, intense hours of work, there was not a person who didn't want to have more of the exciting and affirming interaction that characterized his or her group—that left them changed, energized, connected, and hopeful.

The Promise of Transformation

Early on, our friend, Tom—whom you met in Chapter Two—helped us frame this book. He said, "It's all about magic. It's about creating something really amazing at work. Every day, I do my best to help make that happen." It seems right that as we close, we return to Tom's early comment.

Why did Tom say *magic?* Others we interviewed used that same word. We were taken with the surprise and delight that bubbled forth in our interviews. Something unexpected happens, something that seems miraculous, in a word, magic—and people are drawn to that experience. Something transforming that happens because people have been in a group together. Thanks to all that we've learned while writing this book, the two of us are confident that those magical experiences will happen much more often when group members, leaders, and facilitators pay attention to Group Needs, feelings, and consciously chosen behaviors.

Given all the world's challenges, it would appear that we twenty-first century humans need all the transforming help we can get. And that help comes through joining with others to address our global and community complexities and meet our own very real needs to group.

So go ahead. What are you waiting for? Go out there and find a group. Take a tip from Tom and try for a little transforming magic. See what happens. We suspect you'll be glad you did.

Appendix A

PRACTICE EXERCISES

Since some readers learn best through doing, we offer a set of exercises related to the Self, Group, and World loops and the six Group Needs. As a reminder, here are the definitions of the six Group Needs.

- *Acceptance*: Knowing and accepting ourselves for who we are
- *Potential*: Sensing and growing into our fuller and better selves
- *Bond*: The connections among us that create a shared sense of identity and belonging
- *Purpose*: The reason we come together
- *Reality*: Understanding and accepting the world as it is and how it affects us
- *Impact*: Our intention to make a difference and our readiness to act

Look over the titles of these nine exercises, select one that attracts you, and read through it quickly. See whether it sounds intriguing, different from what you would ordinarily do, and risky within reason. Then try it. The first four exercises can be completed by yourself; the last five involve working with a group. Here are the exercises:

Self-Acceptance and Potential

Exercise 1: See Yourself Through the Model

Exercise 2: Recall a Great Group Experience

Exercise 3: Stretch Toward Your Potential

Group Bond and Purpose

Exercise 4: Build Relationships with Others

Exercise 5: We Are Tribal

Exercise 6: Emerging Group Purpose

World Reality and Impact

Exercise 7: Impact the World Through Groups

Exercise 8: Getting to Know World Reality

Exercise 9: Be the Change You Want

All nine exercises move you toward your better self; make the time to do some of them. And they will have a more lasting effect when you collect your ideas and reflections in a journal.

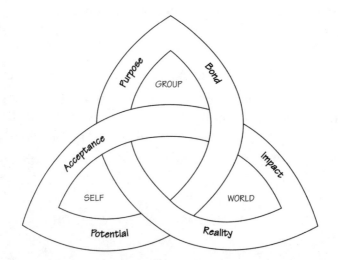

Exercises for Reaching
Self-Acceptance and Potential

Your effectiveness in groups relies on the strengths empha-
sized in the Self loop—accepting who you are and growing
into your Potential.

Exercise 1: See Yourself Through the Model

*Goal: Increase your clarity about what you need from groups and
what you offer to groups.*

A. Return to the Group Needs as shown in the model on the
   previous page. Use the following questions to reflect on
   the six needs. Save your answers in your journal.

   1. Acceptance: What are the abilities, talents, knowl-
      edge, and positive personal characteristics that you
      typically bring to a group? What excites you about
      bringing these abilities? What shortcomings do you
      worry about in a group situation? What concerns you
      about these shortcomings?

   2. Potential: Describe the direction in which you would
      like to grow your talents. What do you need to do in
      your current work and life to experience the growth
      you need? What skills do you have that could be used
      better? How might you use your next new group to
      more intentionally grow yourself?

   3. Bond: What do you want or need from the groups in
      your life? What types of relationships would you like
      to have with other group members? What roles do
      you like to play in groups? What would you like to
      get better at, when it comes to establishing yourself
      in groups?

4. Purpose: What kinds of groups are you attracted to? Why? Comment on how much you are drawn to groups created to have an impact on the world versus groups created to support members.

5. Reality: How would you describe your outlook on life? More or less: positive/negative; hopeful/cynical; optimistic/pessimistic; analytical/emotional? Give examples and reasons. What challenges do you face? What resources support you? What are some of the measures you use to assess how well you are doing in the world? At work? In your personal life?

6. Impact: What kind of differences do you want to make in the world around you? How important is it to you to make such differences? Why? How does this affect the groups you choose to join?

B. You have just looked at the six needs and applied them to yourself. Review your answers and highlight your key points. Consider how these reflections might affect how you would introduce yourself to a new group.

Exercise 2: Recall a Great Group Experience

Goal: Bring to life the notion of an extraordinary group and your contribution to it.

A. Think about a group experience you've had that could be described as amazing, remarkable, exceptional, magical, or really great.

B. Take notes on your answers to these questions:
   1. What factors helped this to be such a wonderful experience?

2. How did you contribute?

3. What was most satisfying or fulfilling? Why?

4. Were you changed because of this experience? If yes, How are you different and how has that difference impacted your life?

C. Reconsider the experience you just described, answering these needs-related questions:

1. What did you learn about yourself?

2. What caused you to grow?

3. What did you like about belonging to the group?

4. How connected were you to the group's Purpose or other members?

5. How did the group pay attention to the world around it? To what effect?

6. When you think of the Impact of the group, what is most satisfying to you?

D. The questions in B above were very general; questions in C were based on the Group Needs model; now go deeper.

1. Describe the difference in your answers to the questions in B and C. What, if anything, did the questions in C call forth beyond those in B?

2. What new understandings, if any, came as a result of the six Group Needs related questions in C.

3. What might you do differently the next time you join a group?

Exercise 3: Stretch Toward Your Potential

Goal: Move yourself to a position that requires you to do something you don't know yet how to do.

A. Think of a group you are currently involved with. Imagine that two years from now you are looking back on your work with this group, feeling proud of what you've learned. List what you are proud of and check the three items you would most like to improve in over two years.

B. Tell your group at least one item from your improvement list. Ask them what you might do and what they could do to help you develop.

C. Look for someone with the capabilities you want to develop. Watch that person at work; how might you engage him or her in coaching you?

D. Ask another group member to be a sounding board for you as you stretch into these new behaviors. Periodically chat with that person about your progress, getting feedback and suggestions. Act on what you hear; notice what happens.

Exercises for Reaching Group Bond and Purpose

These exercises help you and your group-mates better appreciate the melding of Acceptance and Potential with Bond and Purpose. Begin by looking back through your journal for clues on what you and your group might work on.

Exercise 4: Build Relationships with Others

Goal: Explore how you develop relationships with people in your group.

In Chapter Five we suggested that making relationships is akin to making candles. Candles are formed a layer at a time by repeatedly dipping the candle in wax. And so it is with group-based relationships grow slowly over time by repeatedly returning to the group and dipping yourself in. With one group in mind, make notes on your answers to these questions:

A. How would you characterize your relationships with the group as a whole? With individuals in it?

B. Which relationships are closest and most distant? What makes them so? Think more in terms of behavior, rather than personality.

C. What have you done to build bonds with the group and the individuals it? Compare your efforts with those members you feel closer to and more distant from. What one or two things could you do to reinforce the bonds you feel with people you are close to? With those people you feel more distant from?

D. How do your behaviors and feelings with this group fit with other groups in your life—if at all? Are any patterns evident?

E. Save your notes on all of this. Bring them to your next group meeting as a reminder.

Exercise 5: We Are "Tribal"

Goal: Share perspective about the culture of the group and its impact.

The words *tribe* or *clan* inspire images of a tight group of people who depend upon and defend themselves. Tribes usually have mutually understood ways of doing things together. Over time these become more instinctive, habitual, seldom questioned. These are people who truly understand the phrase, "I've got your back."

A. Look up tribe on Wikipedia. Note words used to describe tribe. Which words are you most attracted to?

B. Ask your group what words come to mind when you say *tribe* or *tribal*. Note those and offer the words you collected online.

C. Based on these reflections, ask the group: What might an outsider observe about how we go about doing things? What are our group patterns and habits? How do they serve us? How do they get in our way? Does this discussion suggest we should do anything differently?

Exercise 6: Emerging Group Purpose

Goal: Encourage deeper exploration of group purpose.

It's not unusual for groups to form around a clear and early Purpose and then with time to discover that there is more than what first met the eye. The initial Purpose stands and is not discarded, but members—individually or collectively— find the work takes on new meaning that connects to another, related reason for coming together.

A. Ask members to make a few notes on why your group meets, what it is called together to do.

B. Ask each person to say what she or he holds as the group's Purpose. Discourage discussion between each person's comments.

C. When everyone has spoken, consider what you have heard together.

D. Ask the group whether it needs to reclarify the shared Purpose. If so, find a way together to refine the Purpose and record it for your continuing use in making decisions.

Exercises for Reaching World Reality and Impact

The next three exercises are designed to help groups accept the Reality they face and make change in their world.

Exercise 7: Impact the World Through Groups

Goal: Recognize how you already are connected to making positive change in the world.

A. List the groups that are important in your life. Write down the Purpose of each group.

B. Mark the groups that are about External Change—those that directly intend to make a difference in the world.

C. Mark the Individual Support groups—those committed to making members more effective in the outside world as human beings, as community members, as family members, or as people in the workplace.

D. Notice which groups you are more drawn to, if any. How is your commitment to each group influenced by the way the group impacts the world? Note your observations.

E. What meaning do you take away from these reflections? Discuss this with a friend; ask what he or she thinks this might suggest for your participation in your groups.

F. Go to the next meeting of an important group with your notes and discussion in mind. Say something positive about that group and its Purpose based on your thoughts. Make this a short, simple statement; say it sincerely; don't expect a long conversation about it. Just appreciate the group and let go of it. Notice any reactions.

G. If this goes well, try it again with another group.

Exercise 8: Getting to Know World Reality

Goal: *Identify what your group needs to learn about its world.*

This exercise will work most effectively with External Change groups.

A. Identify an important issue that challenges your group's ability to fulfill its Purpose or achieve its desired Impact. Develop a short statement that defines that issue.

B. Present the issue to the group and ask: What do we need to know in order to meet this challenge? Build a list of the responses; many of them will be in the form of questions.

C. Prioritize the list, considering each item in terms of two characteristics: power to block your group's success and the urgency with which you need to attend to this issue. Items that are particularly powerful and urgent should be among the top priorities.

D. Pick the top three items. For each, develop a strategy to address the concern; identify who in the group will do what by when.

E. In future meetings, return to the plans so that members can report on their actions and discussions can focus on progress or the need to address other issues on the list.

F. Periodically create time for members to reflect on what they are learning about the group's Reality and ways of responding to it.

Exercise 9: Be the Change You Want

Goal: *Cause a group to consider how its internal behavior relates to what it is trying to accomplish in the world.*

This exercise builds on the belief that change in the external world begins within the group.

A. Ask your group: What are we trying to make happen in the world? Build a list of answers. Don't be surprised by the range of responses. Ask people to elaborate on the items with examples that indicate that the desired change has been achieved.

B. Ask: How are we/could we, in our group, be the change that we want to see out there? Discuss how you currently represent the change internally as well as how you don't and might.

C. Based on the discussion, ask some of these additional questions: Is all of this really important? Does it matter that we are consistent with what we are pursuing in the world? What are the consequences of our group acting consistently—or not—with the change we are trying to create? What's the Impact on our group effectiveness? Our Purpose? On group members? On the world we are dealing with? Hear the array of views on these questions.

D. Return to the central question again—in B above—and ask whether, based on discussion, this question deserves any more attention. If it does, ask: What might we do internally that is consistent with the external change we hope to create? If the group reaches agreement about what it wants to do, make sure you do your part to assure appropriate follow-up.

E. In closing, ask members what they have learned from this exploration.

Appendix B

AN OVERVIEW OF EXTRAORDINARY GROUPS

Of all that we've written about, what should you be paying attention to if you want to move your group toward being extraordinary? What should you be reminding yourself of in your day-to-day interactions with your group? What would be useful to you at work, in the moment? We have constructed page 209 with these questions in mind.

This overview gathers our central ideas in a way that is easy to photocopy and take with you. This single page reminds you of what you have read and will want to remember while with a group. We encourage you to make copies of it and share it with others. The overview does not suggest what to do—that's what the book does—but this single page reminds you of what to be looking for during your interactions with your groups and its members.

Possible actions you might take with this one page in hand include:

1. Design your next group meeting with this summary page in mind.

2. Observe a group meeting: How well is your team meeting the six Group Needs and behaving in ways that fit with the indicators of extraordinary groups?

3. When thinking about how a group member might be motivated, assess him or her against the needs, feelings, and behaviors on this summary page.

4. Use the overview to design the steps you will use as you bring a new member into the group.

5. Ask the group to assess itself against the eight indicators.

6. Suggest that group members offer examples of how the six Group Needs and four feelings of transformation are demonstrated in the group.

7. With the overview as a reference, discuss a recent successful project. How did your experience reflect the eight indicators or the six Group Needs? What lessons do you take away from this debrief?

8. Mark this page with a reference tab; as you return to certain chapters, use this summary to reflect on various guidance questions.

Extraordinary Groups: An Overview

Purpose: The reason why we come together

Bond: Connections among us that create a shared sense of identity and belonging

Acceptance: Knowing and accepting ourselves for who we are

Impact: Our intention to make a difference and our readiness to act

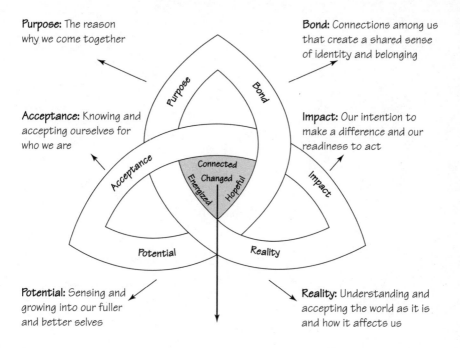

Potential: Sensing and growing into our fuller and better selves

Reality: Understanding and accepting the world as it is and how it affects us

Four Feelings of Transformation

- Did this experience energize you?
- Did you feel more deeply connected to your group or the world around you?
- Did you feel more hopeful about yourself, your group, or the world around you?
- Did you feel changed by this experience?

Indicators of Extraordinary Groups

- Compelling Purpose
- Shared Leadership
- Just-enough Structure
- Full Engagement

- Embracing Differences
- Unexpected Learning
- Strengthened Relationships
- Great Results

Source: *Extraordinary Groups: How Ordinary Teams Achieve Amazing Results.*
Copyright Geoffrey M. Bellman and Kathleen D. Ryan

Appendix C

PRACTICING WHAT WE PREACH

We two have been personal friends and professional colleagues for over twenty-five years. We share a strong Bond built upon our friendship and a mutual compelling Purpose—this book. During our three years of work on *Extraordinary Groups*, we sought to be extraordinary. We intended to transform ourselves, our relationship, our ideas, and our work through this co-authoring. And, we did—often in ways that surprised both of us.

As one small group of two, we worked to meet the six Group Needs we each brought to this project. We observed our behavior and discussed how it was or was not characteristic of extraordinary groups. And we noted our feelings, how and when we each felt energized, connected, hopeful, and changed by the work we have done together. And we have been successful in ways unimagined at the beginning; we wrote quite a different book and in quite a different way than we anticipated. This whole experience has been transforming for each of us; our partnership has been extraordinary in ways we didn't expect and have seldom experienced.

We recently asked ourselves, "What guides your interactions with your co-author on this book?" We each listed our guides, shared the lists with each other, and offer them to you here. As you read them, notice links to Acceptance and Potential, Bond and Purpose, Reality and Impact. Notice the differences in the two lists. And consider how our lists might fit with your own if you were to list what guides you in your interactions with others in one of your groups.

Kathleen's Guides in Working with Geoff

Kathleen has successfully collaborated on two books, is inclined to reach out to others before writing, and outlines what she intends to write before writing.

1. The relationship is most important; we are committed to each other and helping each other be happy and healthy in the whole of our lives.

2. We care equally about our Purpose and both have absolutely positive intentions.

3. Play to Geoff's strengths and interests and minimize the times when I ask him to do things in a way that doesn't fit naturally.

4. Act with a spirit of discovery and exploration—take a few steps, then see what we learn; take the next obvious step and see where that leads; stay open to the creative possibilities that come because he sees things differently than I do.

5. Get things to a point of being good enough to move ahead; avoid perfectionism.

6. When needed, disagree directly and with an open spirit. Share feelings; say what's going on if it's a bad day. Do not be intimidated by his strengths or strength of feelings.

7. When confused or frustrated, ask: How important is this to you? To us? To the book? Give him space; don't over-talk an issue. Short conversations are better for him.

8. When dealing with our differences: Listen for and respond to the feeling underneath the words. How can I help this be good for Geoff? What is it that he wants or needs? What is it that I need?

9. Express appreciation and affection, excitement about the writing and our process. Celebrate, even briefly, milestones.

10. Maintain a sense of humor.

11. In crunch time, deliver; keep commitments.

Geoff's Guides in Working with Kathleen

Geoff has written five books by himself, is inclined to hole up alone and write, and prefers writing without structure to see what will happen.

1. My ego is behind most of my discomfort. What is Ego saying to me?

2. Her motives serve our relationship and our book. Notice when you question this.

3. Reinforce what she brings to the process. Large and small contributions.

4. Our complementary styles feed creativity and disagreement.

5. Her style has worked for her just as well as my style has worked for me.

6. This book is less important than our relationship.

7. A reminder: I have learned so much through our engagement in this process.

8. Watch for patterns in my difficulties. Act on those—first alone and then with her.

9. Notice my need for control. Notice what happens when I let go.

10. Our meetings have been essential in shaping this book.

We two authors, confirmed in our separate experiences and styles, needed something more important than either of us to allow our creative collaboration. What we found is represented in our lists, and the lists are informed by our model. Our work together offered more exhilaration than anguish, but included both. We lived the challenges of embracing differences again and again. And we came through our differences with a deepened appreciation of our book and each other. None of that would have been there without our differences: pulling apart regularly to find our edges preceded pulling together, always first within the Bond of friendship and shared Purpose. Then, supporting each other with Acceptance and Potential, and together reaching toward Reality and Impact.

Appendix D

MORE GROUP RESOURCES

The books, articles, and Web sites below speak of hot spots, communities, social networks, great groups, sparks, tribes, and collective wisdom, all notions related to what we have called extraordinary groups. Each source offers its unique perspective on what can happen among people gathered for common purpose—and what wildly different perspectives they are! Follow your nose, and your Purpose, as you weave these thoughts into what we offered you in our book.

Bennis, Warren, and Biederman, P. W., 1997. *Organizing Genius: The Secrets of Creative Collaboration*. New York: Perseus Books.

> The authors use numerous and prominent corporate stories from recent history to illustrate ten principles common to "great groups"— people who have successfully collaborated for amazing and world-shaping results. Bennis and Biederman's book and our own come to complementary conclusions; their book gives more emphasis to the leader. For a preview of the Bennis book, see the next resource.

Bennis, Warren, Winter/1997. *"The Secrets of Great Groups." Leader-to-Leader*, No. 3, Winter, 1997. http://www.leadertoleader.org/knowledgecenter/journal.aspx?ArticleID=140

> Bennis reviews the ten principles common to great groups and their supporting organizations. One of the world's established leadership experts, he sees groups from the leader's perspective. You will find the six Group Needs we identify lurking behind his ten principles.

Block, Peter, 2008. *Community: The Structure of Belonging*. San Francisco: Berrett-Koehler.

> Block sees small groups as the unit of transformation of the larger community. Community lives first in small groups and expands from there to larger collections of people. Where our book attends more to individual needs in relation to the small group, Block attends more to the small group in relation to the community. His book emphasizes conversation, accountability, commitment, questions, and the design of physical space, all to foster a deep sense of belonging. A provocative and inspiring book.

Collective Wisdom Initiative. http://www.collectivewisdominitiative.org

> A fascinating website for deeper and alternative explorations of group wisdom. Many individuals have contributed to this pursuit of the deeper meaning of collective consciousness. They share a fascination with the important and invisible ways people join for common Purpose. Their exploration delves into how we humans are connected, how we collaborate to create—especially to create wisdom. You can join them at this Web site.

The Community Consulting Partnership. http://www.ccpseattle.org

> In 1996, we helped found this all-volunteer community organization in Seattle. CCP serves the not-for-profit community through consultation to improve organizations' effectiveness. Teams of volunteer consultants learn about consulting by consulting, each team backed by a senior consultant. And nine people at the center of CCP—the "Keepers of the Flame"—make this happen year after year. That small group's success inspired us to write this book. This Web site tells you more about how CCP has served seventy organizations over thirteen years.

Cross, Rob, and Liedtka, J., and Weiss, L. "A Practical Guide to Social Networks." *Harvard Business Review,* March, 2005, pp. 124–132. http://sixdegrees.wdfiles.com/local—files/reading-history/practicalguide.pdf

> Based on Cross's book, *The Hidden Power of Social Networks* (Harvard Business School Press, 2004), this article elaborates on the three informal networks vital to recognizing opportunities or challenges and delivering the necessary response. Where we write about groups within organizations, Cross writes of the elusive social networks that allow organizations to function—often in spite of the formal structure.

Ehrenreich, Barbara, 2006. *Dancing in the Streets: A History of Collective Joy.* New York: Henry Holt.

> Step back to see this large, historic view of the human impulse toward collective celebration and revelry. Ehrenreich looks into communal celebration from the perspective of human biology and culture. Her experience supports our belief that our need to group is first of all instinctual. She gives special attention to the reasons joy has so often been suppressed, causing us to consider the small group in its larger context, the organization.

Fetzer Institute, 2001. *Centered on the Edge—Mapping a Field of Collective Intelligence & Spiritual Wisdom.* http://www.collectivewisdominitiative.org/CenteredOnTheEdge/home.htm

No listed author, publication date, or publisher. The book inspired the creation of the collective wisdom initiative Web site referenced earlier; it flows from surveys and interviews with over one hundred people. The core question: What exactly is this phenomenon when groups touch, or are touched by, the intelligence they need? That intriguing question leads to some surprising answers.

Godin, Seth, 2008. *Tribes: We Need You to Lead Us*. New York: Penguin.

Godin brings tribes into the twenty-first century. His tribes would include our small groups and reach way beyond—to any group of people, large or small, connected to one another, a leader, and an idea. Godin also sees groups and tribes as part of our nature—and that new tribes, tribes of thousands, continue being formed through iPhones and Facebook and My Space.

Gratton, Lynda, 2007. *Hot Spots: Why Some Teams, Workplaces, and Organizations Buzz with Energy—And Others Don't*. San Francisco: Berrett-Koehler.

"Hot Spots" show themselves in ready cooperation, great energy, innovation, and excitement. You will see the parallels between Gratton's work and our own; we are all curious about what allows creativity and productivity to emerge. As the title suggests, her book focuses on creating the event whereas ours attends to the needs of the team. Her book fits most closely with our eight indicators of extraordinary group performance.

Jaworski, J., Flowers, Betty S., and Senge, Peter, 1996. *Synchronicity: The Inner Path of Leadership*. San Francisco: Berrett-Koehler.

We must deepen our understanding of Reality while we shape our collective future—this is just one of the more important points our two books share. This book, along with the Scharmer book described later, brings new perspectives to the study of leadership and change. *Synchronicity* speaks of the world quite differently from how we do in our book, and we find it easy to connect with our Group Needs model.

Lawrence, Paul, and Nohria, N., 2002. *Driven: How Human Nature Shapes Our Choices*. San Francisco: Jossey-Bass.

These Harvard professors reach back 200 years, add recent research from the biological and social sciences, and propose a unified synthesis of human nature. They believe human behavior is guided by four distinct drives: the drives to bond, learn, acquire, and defend. The first two relate directly to our model, and the remaining two we hardly touch upon.

Lencioni, Patrick. *The Five Dysfunctions of Teams* (2002) and *Overcoming the Five Dysfunctions of Teams* (2005). San Francisco: Jossey-Bass.

Both Lencioni's books are built around team dysfunctions: Absence of Trust, Fear of Conflict, Lack of Commitment, Avoidance of Accountability, and Inattention to Results. In many ways, these dysfunctions are the dark mirror of our Group Needs model. He lets you know what you need to watch out for and helps you create the team you want. We give much less attention to what might go wrong and more to what could go right.

Leonard-Barton, Dorothy, and Swap, W. C., 1999. *When Sparks Fly: Harnessing the Power of Group Creativity*. Cambridge: Harvard Business School Press.

Another take on "Hot Spots," *Sparks* speaks to managers seeking maximum creativity from their groups. The book is rich in corporate examples and fits with themes we have written about.

Logan, Dave, King, J., and Fischer-Wright, H., 2008. *Tribal Leadership: Leveraging Natural Groups to Build a Thriving Organization*. New York: Harper Collins.

The authors' work parallels our own with their recognition of humans' genetic predisposition to group. Our book speaks of groups of 2 to 20; their book speaks of tribes of 20 to 150. Our model fits nicely within their views on tribal culture and leadership.

Scharmer, C. Otto, 2009. *Theory U: Leading from the Future as It Emerges*. San Francisco: Berrett-Koehler.

Begin with seeing your world in new ways and new actions will flow from this. Scharmer's book is one of the better examples of seeing the world differently, and in ways that reveal what we have previously been blind to. His Theory U model does just that as it takes us into ourselves, into our willingness to act from what we know, and into our hearts to release solutions already inside us. Scharmer's ambitious perspective reframes how we think about ourselves and each other. A stimulating, challenging book.

Acknowledgments

Over three years, more than one hundred generous people made room for us and our work in their busy lives. We want to thank each and every person and hope that as they read *Extraordinary Groups*, they find a small bit of pride in our collective accomplishment.

Our gratitude goes first to the sixty people we interviewed about their extraordinary group experiences. By sharing their stories, they fed our discoveries and allowed us to speak from their experience. Others passed along our request for interviews and enthusiastically linked us with their friends, colleagues, and family members.

Our primary editors at Jossey-Bass, Genoveva Llosa and Byron Schneider, brought their insight, ability to see concepts and details at once, and belief in our topic. Bernadette Walter brought her marketing savvy and contagious enthusiasm; Mark Karmendy saw us through the production phase with clear guidance and timely responses to our questions. And from early on, as with our past books, Ray Bard of Bard Press listened, asked great questions, provided smart guidance, and told us to go for it!.

Linda Williams, Dorcas Nepple, and Sheila Kelly each read the manuscript at critical times. If they look closely, they will find their influence on our ideas. Claire Ricci, Dee Knapp, and Margaret Dunphy jumped in to assist with our data analysis. Frank Basler and Bud Orr not only edited the manuscript at least twice, they also discussed it with us at length and repeatedly. Bud also helped with our field study interviews.

The Port of Tacoma and the City of Tacoma, two of Kathleen's separate but geographically adjacent clients, provided encouragement and fertile real-world ground for testing our model. She especially thanks the Port's Culture Team and Mary Morrison at the City of Tacoma.

Three talented and tolerant sages—Robert Bashor in Seattle, Robert Fijlstra in Amsterdam, and Robert Henderson in Glasgow—supported, challenged, built upon our ideas over meals, e-mail, and Skype. Geoff is thankful for you three.

We've already mentioned our partners in life, Sheila Kelly and Bud Orr, because of their roles in helping us create this book. We mention them again because of all we have learned from them about extraordinary pairs over the years of our marriages. In our lives, there is no more important grouping than the one Geoff has with Sheila and Kathleen has with Bud.

About the Authors

Geoffrey M. Bellman has worked with large organizations for forty years—fourteen as an internal consultant and manager, twenty-six as an external consultant. His work has focused on renewing large, mature organizations. He serves as faculty for many graduate programs in organization development. In recent years, he has given much of his time to small, not-for-profit organizations in the Seattle area.

Geoff's consultation, workshops and talks have taken him to five continents. He has written six books, with over 250,000 in print and in a dozen languages:

Extraordinary Groups: How Ordinary Teams Achieve Amazing Results. San Francisco: Jossey-Bass, 2009. With co-author, Kathleen D. Ryan.

The Consultant's Calling: Bringing Who You Are to What You Do. San Francisco: Jossey-Bass, 2002. For those who want to know what consulting is really like as a career, as a living, and as a life.

Getting Things Done When You Are Not in Charge. San Francisco: Berrett-Koehler, 2001. The title says it all.

The Beauty of the Beast: Breathing New Life into Organizations. San Francisco: Berrett-Koehler, 2000. What we love to hate about organizations and how to change them.

Your Signature Path: Gaining New Perspectives on Life and Work. San Francisco: Berrett-Koehler, 1996. Balancing work, family, community, and life while facing an uncertain future.

The Quest For Staff Leadership. Glencoe: Scott-Foresman, 1986. For managers of staff functions in large organizations everywhere.

Geoff is a founder of the Community Consulting Partnership and the Woodlands Group. He has been honored by the Organization Development Network and the Whidbey Institute for his contributions to his profession and the community.

Find more of Geoff's writing on www.scribd.com or www. facebook.com

You can reach Geoff at geoffbellman@gmail.com

Kathleen D. Ryan has practiced organization development since 1984 through the Orion Partnership, a consulting firm she cofounded with her husband, Bud Orr. Identified as "an organizational consultant with an instinct for translating complex human behavior into practical concepts," she guides her clients through executive on-boarding and coaching, culture change, and team and leadership development. She has content expertise in trust, collaboration, fear, risk taking, interpersonal communications, group dynamics, conflict management and organization development. She regularly speaks at conferences, professional association meetings, and corporations.

Kathleen has consulted with a wide range of clients in various profit and not-for-profit sectors, including telecommunications, aerospace, manufacturing, technology, health care, government, education, philanthropy, and human services. Publications include

Extraordinary Groups: How Ordinary Teams Achieve Amazing Results. San Francisco: Jossey-Bass, 2009. With co-author Geoffrey M. Bellman.

Driving Fear Out of the Workplace: Creating the High-Trust, High-Performance Organization. San Francisco: Jossey-Bass, 1990, 1998; 2nd edition. With co-author Daniel Oestreich. Recognized as 1990 Book of the Year by the Society for Human Resource Management.

The Courageous Messenger: How to Successfully Speak Up at Work . San Francisco: Jossey-Bass, 1996. Co-authored with Daniel Oestreich and George (Bud) Orr. Guidance for anyone who wants to effectively raise sensitive issues that feel risky.

Many chapters for books on managing change, organization transformation, building trust, and the connection between accountability and commitment.

Kathleen has many groups in her life, not the least of which are two women's groups and a personal-professional development group with four other consultants. Like Geoff, she is a cofounder of the Community Consulting Partnership. She serves on the board of directors for Seattle University's master's degree program in Organizational Design and Renewal.

Kathleen can be reached at orionpartnership@comcast .net or through www.orionpartnership.com.

Index

transformation in, 55–56; examining beliefs about, 150; examples of extraordinary, 6–11; facilitating, 95–96; facing adversity and resistance, 118–120; forming, 181–184; ground rules for, 163; group identity and Bond, 83–84, 145; helping others embrace differences, 156–165; how transformations happen in, 53–56, 124; human need for, 33–34, 192; identifying outside influences on, 180–181; importance of small, 14–16; issues of space and control in, 154–156; keeping together, 120–122; leadership for, 168; lightness and humor in, 96–98; linking Purpose to goals, 171; maintaining positive bias toward, 149–151; needing each other to make Impact, 111; playing part in, 84–85; potential of, 191–192; preparing individuals to embrace, 147–156; refreshing meeting design, 162; setting goals for, 116–117; shifting roles within, 162–163; six needs of, 34–35; structures to hold differences, 161–165; studying dynamics of, 4–6; understanding power of, 111; value of differences in, 139–140; working through differences, 144–147. See also Extraordinary groups; Facilitating groups

Growth, 66–67

H

Head and heart, 54
Hopeful feelings, 49, 51–52
Human needs: need for groups, 33–34, 192; paired in Group Needs model, 34–35
Humor: contributing in group, 96–98; in extraordinary groups, 25–26

I

Icons of Group Needs model, 13
Impact: Bond and Purpose joined with, 131–132; defined, 43; in Group Needs model, 12, 35, 42–44, 112–113; improving the world, 110–111; as key to transformation, 53–54; naming larger, 170–171; needing each other to make, 111; overview of, 106–107; Potential and

Purpose joined with, 132–134; setting group goals, 116–117; statements reflecting, 110–111; understanding power of group, 111; using intention and action for, 146–147. See also Reality

Improving the world, 110–111
Individual Support groups, 22, 106
Individuals: accepting Reality and Impact, 145–147; benefits of extraordinary groups to, 15–16; bonding with groups, 125–128, 245; counting on each other, 87–88; embracing group differences, 147–156; focusing on strengths, 74–75; fulfilling potential, 66, 70–72, 145; gaining sense of identity and belonging, 83–84, 145; influencing each other, 87; knowing and appreciating self, 144–145; maintaining positive bias toward group, 149–151; moving in same direction, 87; need for learning and growth, 66–67; personal ease of, 64–65; personal nature of transformation, 55; playing our parts in groups, 84–85; responding to Group Needs of, 159–161; space and control issues for, 154–156; strengthened with group Bond, 128–129; taking risks, 113–116, 153–154; transformation of, 54–55; transformative effects of groups on, 60–61

J

Journals, 13

K

Keeping groups together, 120–122

L

Leadership: about group, 168; collaborative, 22–23, 182; discussing group differences, 175–178; facilitative, 168–169; framing inspiring Purpose, 170–172; leaders in extraordinary groups, 188–189; light touch for, 172–175; managing world around group, 178–181; selecting right team, 181–184; style of, 174. See also Facilitating groups